Fashion Desi₵
Product Develoμ...

Fashion Design and Product Development

Harold Carr and John Pomeroy

Blackwell
Science

© 1992 by Harold Carr and John Pomeroy

Blackwell Science Ltd, a Blackwell Publishing company

Editorial Offices:
Blackwell Science Ltd, 9600 Garsington Road, Oxford OX4 2DQ, UK
     Tel: +44 (0) 1865 776868
Blackwell Publishing Inc., 350 Main Street, Malden, MA 02148-5020, USA
     Tel: +1 781 388 8250
Blackwell Science Asia Pty, 550 Swanston Street, Carlton, Victoria 3053, Australia
     Tel: +61 (0)3 8359 1011

First published 1992 by Blackwell Science Ltd
Reprinted 1996, 1997, 2001, 2003, 2006

ISBN-10: 0-632-02893-9
ISBN-13: 978-0-632-02893-1

Library of Congress Cataloging-in-Publication Data
Carr, Harold
    Fashion design and product development/by Harold Carr and John Pomeroy
        p.   cm.
    Includes bibliographical references and index.
    ISBN 0-632-02893-9
    1. Fashion design.   2. New Products–Management.   I. Pomeroy, John.   II. Title.
TT507.C353 1992
746.9′2′0685 – dc20   92-21693
                                                                                      CIP

A catalogue record for this title is available from the British Library

Set by SNP Best-set Typesetter Ltd., Hong Kong

For further information on Blackwell Publishing, visit our website:
www.blackwellpublishing.com

Figures 6.1, 6.3, 6.4, 6.14 and 6.15 are extracts from the British Standards 3870: 1982 and 1983
Schedule of Stitches and Seams, and are reproduced by kind permission of the British Standards
Institution, 389 Chiswick High Road, London W4 4AL, from whom complete copies can be
obtained.

Contents

Preface

The aim of this book is to present fashion design as a commercial activity. Therefore the book does not contain illustrations of past or present fashion concepts. Nor do the authors seek to prescribe what makes fashion ideas in themselves successful or unsuccessful. There are many other books which attempt to do this. What this book attempts to show is how the process of design and product development within a company tests, changes and refines fashion ideas, be they original, adapted or copies.

When the authors use the word design, they imply a process which begins with market research, to identify the need for a style or garment product, and ends only when the company has manufactured and sold the last garment. The challenge of market research first of all produces a visual response: a story board, a fashion sketch or draping fabric around models. To create samples and manufacture garments, however, requires a complex interaction of many themes.

The designer must select the fabric and trims, which not only average half the total cost of manufacture but are also an intimate part of the design concept, if not the primary stimulus and feature of the design. The designer should play a part in the design of the process which manufactures the styles, in order to ensure that the factory has the competence to copy the design image faithfully, and to prevent busy industrial engineers throwing the baby out with the bath water. The designer's decisions determine fabric usage and the work content of the style, together the basis of direct costs. The designer should argue with cost accountants and production managers in order to define accurately the adaptations needed to reduce the cost of manufacturing and make a profit at a given price. The designer should know from the beginning the implications of a new style for capital investment decisions and the costs of training. The designer should realise the influence of design decisions on the lead time for fabric delivery and hence production planning and delivery schedules. The designer is responsible for quality of design and also indirectly for quality of conformity, the ease with which operators avoid defects.

The information coming from inspection in the factory feeds back to the designer the success or failure of the design in manufacture; and returns from customers feed back to the designer the shortcomings of the design in the market. The success of the designer is reflected in the volume of sales, the perceived value which underpins the price, and thus the contribution to fixed overheads and profits which provides the means by which the company thrives.

Organisation is simply defined as the division of work into tasks which can be performed by one person, and the provision of the means of co-ordination. No one person can carry out all the tasks of design and product development in a large company. How the tasks are divided among the members of the team and how their work is co-ordinated, planned and controlled is crucial for the success of the company. The authors do not wish to fight over the meaning of words. Referring to the above paragraph, some companies may confine the meaning of the word *designer* to those who provide the initial visual response to the challenges of market research. The title then given to the manager of the process of design and product development may be 'Managing Director', 'Marketing Director', 'Design Manager', 'Garment Technologist', and so on. What is important is comprehensive management of the process, because the process is both unitary and iterative.

The justification for this book is the authors' failure to find a similar text available in English. Much of the material used in this book is available dispersed throughout many books and articles in journals, which are acknowledged in Further Reading. The authors' main aim has been to construct a connected story of design and product development for the clothing industry.

We wish to thank the library staff at the London College of Fashion, and especially Barbara Smith, for continuous support in the search for relevant texts.

We thank the British Standards Institution for permission to abstract relevant codes and diagrams from British Standards; these are acknowledged in detail in the text.

We thank especially Richard Miles for perceiving the need for this book and having the patience to encourage its writing.

Harold Carr
John Pomeroy

1

The Process and Structure of the Industry

The business of fashion and clothing manufacture broadly has seven stages:

Fibre production
↓
Yarn production
↓
Weaving or knitting
↓
Dyeing and finishing
↓
Garment manufacture
↓
Retailing
↓
Consumption

In some contexts, taking the description beyond fibre production might seem appropriate, but both the manufacture of basic chemicals and the preparation and maintenance of land for sheep grazing respond more to long term economic forces than to the shorter term demands of fashion. Indeed the demands of fashion tend to become more imperative the further down the chain the product progresses. Goods pass down the chain and information passes in both directions. In general terms each stage comprises a number of independent companies competing for business with the next stage. Some larger companies manage undertakings in more than one stage, more often acting as a conglomerate than in the sense of vertical integration.

The total time lag from fibre production to goods sold in retail stores varies perhaps from six to 18 months. A typical pipeline, in one recent analysis, comprised 66 weeks: 23 weeks at the fibre and textile stages, 24 weeks in garment manufacture and 19 weeks in retailing.

The feedback of information which controls fashion, price, volume of output and quality standards is primarily the rate of consumer purchasing. The information flow on fashion, price and volume is relatively rapid to the garment manufacturer, and thence to the textile and fibre stages, according to the length of the garment manufacturer's planning cycle. The information time lag on quality standards relating to a new product has in the past been as long as two years to some parts of the chain.

With a new product, such as permanent press in the 1960s, initial standards had to be set fairly arbitrarily, although with all the integrity and expertise of which the producer was capable. Feedback had to occur several times before quality standards were satisfactorily set. In the UK the influence of the large retailing organisations has generally speeded up and expanded this feedback. They can exercise control of garment manufacturers and textile producers, because their knowledge of consumers' wants in terms of quality and reliability is sufficiently advanced.

In addition, at least one large fibre producer, in order to exploit the market effectively, had to set up, successively, research and development services for spinning, weaving and garment manufacture. These services were able to isolate technical problems and provide solutions leading to acceptance of the fibre by all links in the chain. Sometimes the clothing industry itself has a less clear idea of what its customers want. Since it can afford to do little of its own research, the clothing industry is influenced very often by the ideas of the fibre producers and the price and turnover needs of the retailers.

Quality and reliability in clothing depend on factors such as stitch density, seam turnings, seam strengths, amount of elasticity and so on. In quality control language, these are referred to as *variables*, items which can be measured to some extent within the normal meaning of that term. But in the main, especially in areas where fashion plays the most important part, quality is concerned with *attributes*, items which cannot be measured in any normal sense. These are matters of judgement such as general appearance, symmetry, drape or how much the garment enhances the wearer's personality or social status. It is almost always the attributes which sell a garment.

Marketing planning

Two strategies of planning may be identified.

Within the framework of market competition

A company can plan to serve the market more efficiently by anticipating market behaviour and responding to it by buying machinery and materials, by recruiting labour and by stimulating appropriate product development in an attempt to meet market needs. Many small and medium sized clothing manufacturing companies appear to do just this.

To reduce or control market competition

A company can plan in the sense of obtaining the prices, costs and both the consumer and producer responses it wants. This aims to replace the market. This second strategy of planning deals with the unreliability of competitive markets in one or more of four ways:

(1) *Diversification* takes place by the development of ranges in other garment products. The trouser manufacturer makes suits; the swimwear manufacturer makes dresses; the jeans manufacturer begins with trousers, then converts denim into waistcoats, skirts, dresses and jackets, then moves on to other fabrics. Alternatively the manufacturer of one garment product increases his range by taking over companies making other garment types, which he feels he can manage.

(2) *Replacement of the market* takes place by superseding it through vertical integration. The planning company controls the producer or consumer in order to reduce an unmanageable uncertainty. The idea of vertical integration between clothing manufacturing and clothing retailing has been, with some exceptions, unfashionable since the breakdown of the large vertically integrated menswear organisations in the 1960s and 1970s. This breakdown stemmed largely from the inability of the factory bureaucracies to supply the retail shops with what they could sell, a failure of flexibility in the face of swiftly changing demands, and the failure to meet a price in the face of low cost imports. Yet these organisations retained a rump of owned manufacturing capacity.

Vertical integration lives on in other forms and in other areas. A number of large retail organisations, while owning no manufacturing capacity, effectively control many of their producers: by the transfer into production of managers imbued with the spirit of the retail enterprise, by the pressure exerted through the provision of more sophisticated technological advice, by insisting on detailed manufacturing specifications being met, and not least by the lure of long term contracts. These producers are often spread throughout areas of the developing world and the EC as well as the UK. Again the growth of large textile conglomerates has often built a bridge between cloth manufacturers and clothing manufacturers, which not only brings economies to the chain of production but has also developed more power for negotiating effectively with the large retail organisations.

(3) *Control of the market* takes place by reducing the independence of action of those to whom the planning company sells or from whom it buys, although outwardly competition reigns. One retail chain's decision to buy or not to buy will be very important to its suppliers if it controls say 40% of the market in two significant clothing products. The decision may be a matter of survival for them. Control of price may also be involved because size in the market may enable a buyer to set prices knowing that no individual producer can force a change of price by withdrawing his supply. Competitors may be reluctant to initiate price reductions because this leads to retaliatory price reductions, a situation in which the bigger firms usually win. The amount sold may also be controlled, through advertising, an effective sales organisation and efficient management of design and product development to help ensure customer purchases. One company's designs in knitwear do not necessarily reflect the current fashion, but they are the current fashion when they account for over 40 per cent of the market. The control is necessarily imperfect but important for reducing, although not eliminating, market uncertainty.

(4) *Supervision of the market* takes place for varying lengths of time through use of contracts between seller and producer. In the marketing of clothing it is not possible to determine how large is the proportion governed by the matrix of contracts by which companies reduce market uncertainty for themselves and others. A large contract over a long period is relatively reliable.

On the other hand there exists a serious brake on the kind of planning and control outlined above. The clothing industry is a fashion industry, largely an industry of small production units (even if organised sometimes in larger undertakings), which have the necessary flexibility to meet the inherent demands for change. This small firm economy requires relatively simple products made from simple equipment from readily available materials by a flexible labour force. The period of production is short. The market readily provides the factors of production.

The opposite of this is the world of the technologist and engineer who provide the specialisation of people and manufacturing process, and demand a much larger commitment of time and capital, which together require reliability in the market leading to its control. There is as yet no strong technological imperative in clothing manufacture which would of itself demand a more reliable market.

The technological environment of product development

The technology of clothing divides into three parts: how materials fulfil the aesthetic, functional and commercial requirements of garments; how garments fulfil the social, psychological and functional requirements of those who wear them; and how cutting, sewing, fusing and pressing combine to produce these garments. The aim of fashion design and product development is to integrate the three parts of this technology to originate, extend or adapt garment styles which compete effectively in the clothing marketplace.

Materials

Garments typically comprise a main or outer material, with often an interlining, sometimes a lining, fastenings and surface decoration. The material is in most cases a fabric web which is woven, knitted or non-woven, but which can be a sheet of animal skin or plastic. Fastenings include metal or plastic in zips and a wide range of materials both natural and man-made in buttons and other fastenings. Surface decoration includes embroidery, leather, metal and plastics. All these materials are selected to fulfil design objectives. Correctly chosen materials enhance the design; inappropriate choices create dissatisfied customers and difficulties in manufacture.

One aesthetic objective of materials involves colour. Colour has three properties: hue, such as redness or blueness; value, darkness or lightness; and intensity or pureness. Colour is complicated by other characteristics which affect appearance such as texture (plain versus twill), lustre (shiny versus dull), pattern (checks and prints) and directionality (piles and suedes).

Another objective involves the hand or handle of the fabric, which comprises ideas such as smoothness (as in cashmere), crispness (from hard, strongly twisted yarns), stiffness, spring and fullness (from bulk and richness). These properties relate to the way fabrics drape and cling on the wearer, and the way fabrics move when the wearer moves. One functional objective is sewability or tailorability, which also relates very closely to hand characteristics. Another is shrinkage, which is necessary in woollen tailored garments, but not in an excessive or inconsistent amount if the output is to maintain consistent sizing. Again fabrics have to retain their characteristics after either washing or dry-cleaning.

Fabrics must also meet standards of comfort, which include insulation from loss of body heat, the dissipation of perspiration through wicking and the passage of water vapour after evaporation. Finally all materials may have to resist the action of agents which cause them to deteriorate: sunlight, rubbing against various surfaces including itself, rainwater, body fluids and detritus and, in the case of swimwear, chlorine, brine and sun-tan oil. The important point is to define these agents for each garment type.

There are two chief commercial considerations: the price of materials, especially since material cost is typically half the total cost of manufacture, and sourcing, to ensure a sufficient supply at the right time, in the right quantity at the right quality.

Fashion design

One of the most important factors which differentiates humans from other animals is their use of clothing. It is used not simply to provide a micro-climate for the wearer's body, but also to conceal the body and reveal its wearer's status and personality to others. To satisfy this concealing and revealing process diverse kinds of clothing are used.

One of the most mysterious aspects of clothing is fashion. Anthropologists, psychologists and sociologists have all attempted to analyse this concept, but for the purpose of this book the best that can be said is that fashion appears to be a social process in which some people begin by adopting the image of people unlike themselves. Those in the same sector of society tend to emulate their distinctive appearance, with publicity in the media playing its part, as mentioned later, until the differentiation disappears and the process begins all over again in the search for new appearances.

Clothing expresses status; social class is apparent in the boss's business suit and the worker's jeans at work, although this difference may disappear at the weekend. Clothing changes when the wearer leaves the cradle, enters primary school, secondary school or university, on starting work, on getting married, on gaining promotion. Even death has a special wardrobe, both for the dead and the mourners. Clothing establishes a person's identity; reflects the wearer's goals and moral principles; communicates self-assurance or the lack of it; and conveys the activity a person is about to engage in. Clothing may also be used as costume, to represent something a person is not; and as a uniform to denote a person's membership of a defined group.

The task of a designer is to represent fashion objectives in a sketch which then forms an instruction to the pattern cutter. The pattern cutter cuts a set of patterns which interprets the style and represents the component parts of the garment. The outlines of the patterns are then, in one of several ways, transferred to the fabric so that the garment components may be cut out and assembled into complete garments.

While pattern technology comprises many elements of judgement and creativity, it is also the first time in the design process that measurements and quantities become crucial.

Clothing manufacture

The central process in clothing manufacture is sewing, which subordinates cutting, fusing and pressing to its demands. The sewing machine is the typical item of production equipment in a clothing factory, but the sewing machine is no more than a power operated needle with other mechanisms in synchronisation, which produces a series of stitches continuously. All the rest is left to the operator. The operator controls the shape of the sewing line and hence the shapes of the finished garment. The operator controls the fitting of one ply against another. The operator controls the speed of stitch formation. In addition the operator must interpret instructions on a work ticket about different styles, and be able to judge quality during and after the operation. Thus, apart from perhaps 5–10 per cent of operations where some form of automatic machine can be used, operations in clothing manufacture are largely operator-controlled. The same conditions, in different ways, apply to pressing, but less to cutting.

The operator using a sewing machine produces low added value, because the operator is limited to using only one machine. In addition the machine's output is limited by the practical mechanical constraints of stitch formation, as well as the machine speed the operator can effectively use, especially on short bursts of sewing.

Even this is not nearly as significant as the fact that, however sophisticated the engineering of stitch formation, its technology occupies only about one-fifth of the time of the average sewing operation. The other four-fifths of the time are occupied in activities such as preparing the fabric to be sewn, trimming, folding, creasing, marking, disposal after sewing and bundling. These activities are often referred to as ancillary handling. In fact they are the core of the typical sewing operation, and they have not yet in general been mechanised (although at least three of the world's economies are providing a large investment to break this dependence on the human hand). The only serious inroads into an essentially hand-controlled manufacturing process have taken place in cutting, some pressing and a small minority of sewing operations.

The reasons for the continuing dominance of the human hand stem from the nature of the raw materials, from the nature of the sewing process itself and from the following characteristics of the market:

- Fabrics are limp. Wood and metals expand and contract, causing just as much difficulty to their users as stretching and shrinking in fabrics. This is not the prime difficulty, however. What is crucial is that fabrics bend in all directions. It is therefore much more difficult and expensive to invent jigs and automatic equipment for performing sewing operations than it is for operations on rigid materials.
- Fabrics vary in extensibility. A certain minimum extensibility of yarn is necessary in order that the needle may penetrate the fabric satisfactorily. Both extensibility less than the minimum and very high extensibility give trouble in making up. This extensibility varies not only from fabric to fabric but also according to the angle between the line of sewing and the lengthwise grain of the fabric.
- Fabrics vary in thickness. It is well known that sewing very thin fabrics is more difficult. Perhaps even greater difficulties arise from the varying thicknesses which are handled by one operator or fed through one machine.
- No satisfactory general alternative to sewing has yet been developed because the joining must achieve compatibility with the flexibility, drape and handle of fabrics. In mechanical terms a stitch is a flexible universal joint, the only type of joint whose properties approach those of the fabric.
- A basic theme of the clothing industry is fashion, resulting in much variety and frequency of change. A permutation of the number of styles, sizes and fabrics per season in one factory may easily produce a total of several thousand items. If it were possible to imagine a factory output of one style, one size and one fabric, it is more likely that the problems of mechanisation would have been solved in spite of the physical difficulties.

The production environment

While the simplicity of the sewing machine enables it to provide the required flexibility to cope with ever changing fashion needs, the sewing machine is relatively unproductive. In economic terms, manufacture using sewing machines is usually described as labour intensive or having low added value per operator. Added value is the value added to the cost of raw materials by the manufacturer, or the difference between the value of sales and the value of materials and services purchased. The average added value per operator for clothing manufacture is the lowest for any manufacturing industry.

With low added value per operator, the number of employees other than operators whom a company can support is relatively low. Thus the number of administrative personnel is low and management hierarchies are relatively undeveloped, with managers commonly carrying out many functions, most of them related to the day-to-day running of the business. The relatively late development of the work study function in clothing factories, in spite of obvious economic justifications, and the almost total absence of company based research into garment making processes provide further evidence of this.

A further effect is low capitalisation per operator. Capital expenditure per employee in clothing manufacture throughout the EC was $250 in 1980. Thus entry into the industry is relatively easy. A new entrepreneur primarily needs design flair, a niche in the market and some working capital, but only a small amount of fixed capital. This is why the clothing industry includes a plethora of small firms for which there is always opportunity, and which supply the variety of fashion demanded in the marketplace. This situation ensures the continual introduction of fresh competition throughout much of the clothing market.

Another result of the low output of sewing machine operators in economic terms is the high proportion of labour cost within total cost, usually within a range of 20–25 per cent. The manufacturer tends to compete by keeping labour costs low and achieving a high output from a given labour force. The manufacturer's limiting resource is invariably sewing room labour, whose costs are about 95 per cent of total labour costs. All this leads to pressure on the productivity of sewing room labour and on labour cost.

Throughout the industry the economics of their situation drives companies to employ low priced labour. Approximately 80 per cent of the total labour force is women, largely concentrated in the sewing room. This has occurred because, in spite of equal pay laws, women on average receive about three-quarters of the pay received by men in clothing manufacture. Similarly, clothing manufacturers recruit strongly among school leavers, because young employees during training earn less than older employees. Again the industry employs a relatively high proportion of recent immigrants, a tendency evident at least since the arrival of the Huguenots in the 17th century. The industry includes a number of outworkers and homeworkers, in a complex web of sub-contracting.

Finally the search for low labour cost has led to finding sources of production in factories in countries where the level of wages is lower than in Western Europe. The first industry to develop was in Hong Kong, whose clothing industry now employs almost as many as are employed in the UK. Later Korea, Malaysia and Sri Lanka developed clothing industries, and the latest major arrival on the clothing scene is

Table 1.1 Comparative breakdown of costs.

	USA (%)	Far East (%)
Labour and overheads	50	15
Materials	50	44
Manufacturer's margin	–	5.5
Freight, duty, etc	–	35.5
Cost of goods sold	100	100

India. The USA stimulated development in Puerto Rico, then other Caribbean countries and South America. There are sizeable clothing industries in Tunisia and Malta. Western European countries have also gone to sources in the countries of Eastern Europe. Staple garments with long runs tend to be the favourite products sourced in overseas factories, because the pipeline from design concept to receipt of garments in retail shops can afford to be that much longer. Fashion garments, dependent on the interactions of a metropolitan centre, and requiring a much shorter pipeline, are often still made in the home industry.

Research carried out in 1981 showed the comparative breakdown given in Table 1.1.

An important implication of the figures shown in this table is that a cost reduction of 30 per cent through higher labour productivity would produce a reduction in total cost of 15 per cent in the USA and of only 4.5 per cent in the Far East. This, in a simplified form, provides the justification for the international drive to mechanise clothing operations.

Somewhat fewer than 190 000 people are employed in clothing manufacture in the UK; about 150 000 in retail distribution; a few still in wholesale distribution; about 150 000 in textile manufacture (for all end uses).

About 5500 establishments manufacture clothing; 80 per cent of these employ fewer than 50 people but about 500 of the establishments account for 75 per cent of the output by value.

Employment in clothing has been in continuous decline since 1951 when 550 000 were employed, reflecting largely a continuous rise in imports but also a substantial rise in the productivity of labour (by three-quarters for instance between 1978 and 1983). Roughly 20 per cent of output is exported; but over 50 per cent of consumption, a much larger figure, is imported.

Figure 1.1 shows the industry in the context of the industries which supply it, Fig. 1.2 in the context of industries which use similar technologies.

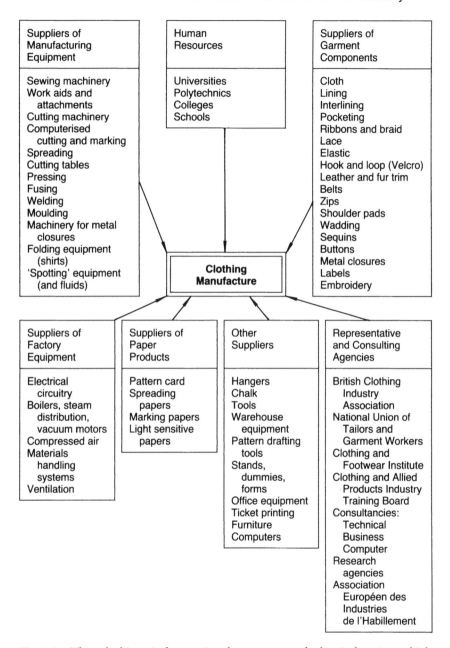

Fig. 1.1 The clothing industry in the context of the industries which supply it.

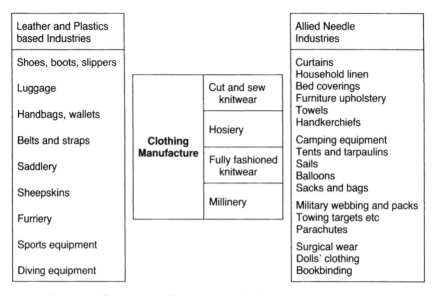

Leather and Plastics based Industries			Allied Needle Industries
Shoes, boots, slippers			Curtains
			Household linen
Luggage		Cut and sew knitwear	Bed coverings
			Furniture upholstery
Handbags, wallets			Towels
		Hosiery	Handkerchiefs
Belts and straps	**Clothing Manufacture**		Camping equipment
			Tents and tarpaulins
Saddlery		Fully fashioned knitwear	Sails
			Balloons
Sheepskins			Sacks and bags
		Millinery	Military webbing and packs
Furriery			Towing targets etc
			Parachutes
Sports equipment			Surgical wear
			Dolls' clothing
Diving equipment			Bookbinding

Fig. 1.2 The context of industries which use similar technologies.

The process of product development

Figure 1.3 shows in diagram form the process of product development.

Market research draws from a world-wide series of shows, representing the work of the most innovative designers; from fashion journals; from style and colour forecasting services; from the garments of competitors; and from the ideas of buyers in retail stores. The *design concept* is developed by drawing (one notable exception was Christian Dior, who wrapped cloth around live models), and a series of trials to refine the ideas of shape, colour and surface decoration. *Market screening* checks the existence of a target population and what segment of the market the concept aims at.

The creation of a *prototype pattern* is a design activity, based on the technology of block patterns or modelling, taking into account research into anthropometrics, in relation to figure types in the market segment, and materials technology. The construction of a first *sample* by a skilled sample machinist explores by what means the garment can be constructed and adjusts the garment to achieve a satisfactory fit. The *range meeting* examines the design concept critically through the medium of a garment for the first time, against initial estimates of material and labour cost and possible contribution to overhead and profit. The range meeting also chooses those garments which are to progress to further development. This meeting is very often the key decision-making point in the whole process, and its members include

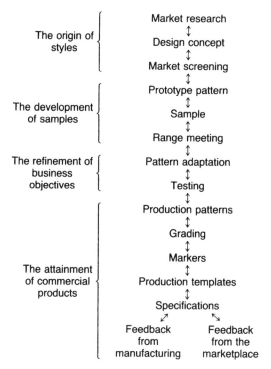

Fig. 1.3 The process of design and product development.

representatives of marketing and production management as well as the design team.

Pattern adaptation, following the decisions of the range meeting, makes alterations to the pattern to correct any fitting problems, to examine opportunities for cost reduction if required, and to resample in alternative fabrics. The results often return to a further range meeting. At this point it is necessary to plan the sequence of construction to be used in bulk production of the new style. From this, proposals for the purchase of new machinery required to manufacture the new style and an estimate of the retraining time required are evaluated. The investment has to be recovered from the predicted sales revenue generated by the style. Production planning then makes estimates of output, according to differing resources which may be used, and sets up possible delivery schedules following a starting date.

The world of *testing* covers an enormous range of objectives: the physiology of 'comfort', resistance to attack by fluids and sunlight, resistance to wear and behaviour in washing and dry-cleaning.

Production patterns include seams, inlays and turnups, grain lines and pattern identification. *Grading*, using information from sizing surveys, increases or decreases the dimensions of the pattern from the sample size until all the sizes in the range are covered. The size range depends on the target market. *Marker making* is crucial because it brings the patterns to the fabric, confined in a rectangle whose width is the fabric width and whose length is as short as possible. Here further adaptations to the patterns may take place in order to make a more efficient marker and reduce the usage of fabric. At the same time pattern cutters, working with production engineers, devise *production templates* for use in factory workplaces on such jobs as buttonhole marking, to aid in the rapid achievement of accuracy. The designer finalises the *specifications* of the requirements of the design. These may have been developed from a fairly early stage.

Feedback from manufacturing may be based initially on a test batch, if the style is radical enough to demand one, but of course is continuous throughout the life of the style. Similarly, *feedback from the marketplace* may also be based on test marketing and is continuous throughout the life of the style. Product development does not cease until the last garment is made and sold.

The above description sets up a typical model of product development for womenswear manufacture. The arrows in Fig. 1.3 indicate that feedback may take place from any stage in the process to any other stage. The members of a product development team should be open-minded flexible individuals, who live to solve problems. The management of such a team brings together the creative and open-ended thinkers, the solvers of defined problems and the financial analysts. This diversity brings special problems to the management of the team.

Some manufacturers of washing machines in the past would develop a new washing machine and then call in the designers to make it look pretty; in the opposite way some clothing manufacturers require their designers to sketch pretty frocks and then leave the rest of the designing to the co-operation of pattern cutters and production engineers. A proper view of clothing design embraces aesthetics, ergonomics applied to fit and fabric, the choice of construction methods (stitch and seam types and the chemistry of fusible resins) and target costs and selling prices. Design is a planning process which begins by being open and creative, but later passes to solving defined problems.

Quick Response

Quick Response is providing the garments the customer wants in the right place, at the right time and at the right price. It depends on integrating all parts of the clothing pipeline (fibre producers, fabric manufacturers, clothing manufacturers and retail stores) in one overall organisation totally responsive to the consumer. What drives and motivates Quick Response is rapid transfer of information among all parts of the pipeline, especially from the point of sale in retail stores back up the pipeline. Quick Response needs open interchange between supplier and customer in all parts of the pipeline. It uses modern computerised technology to achieve the required speed of transfer of information.

Quick Response has a significant impact on three areas: Electronic Data Interchange, Computer Aided Design and the sewing room. The last two are within the clothing manufacturing company, where the company must respond rapidly to information and orders from the customer.

Electronic Data Interchange (EDI)

Here customers and suppliers throughout the industry agree a standardised computer architecture, leading among other items to bar-coding of fabric and garments. Currently the leading exponents in the USA are the Textile Apparel Linkage Council (TALC) and the Voluntary Inter-Industry Communications Standards Committee (VICS). European clothing industries are beginning to develop similar systems.

TALC deals with formats, fabric piece identification, dimensions of pieces, shade measurement, identification of defects and the status of the order. VICS deals with standard item identification. It aims to get agreement among retailers and manufacturers about electronic methods of identifying garments so that automated point of sale equipment can be used to capture precise information on consumer purchases at the Stock Keeping Unit (SKU). For garments this means type, style, fabric, colour, size and special features. The grocery industry has used bar-coding with tracking at electronic point of sale (EPOS) for some years, but the number of suppliers and SKUs it controls is much smaller than the number in the clothing industry. In addition VICS develops standard ways of making the enormous amount of information available at the point of sale useful to the store buyer and the supplier, in order to make the rapid re-ordering of garments easier.

Computer Aided Design (CAD)

CAD in textiles is now highly sophisticated and precise, making the design process rapid and cheap because actual samples are not required as early or as frequently. CAD for clothing is much harder to achieve, but there are a growing number of systems which can contribute to the initial design, substantially in the case of very simple garments. In translating the initial design into two dimensional patterns much has been achieved, but much more remains to be done. Once a prototype pattern has been produced CAD has a much bigger role, in pattern adaptation and grading. Further, computerised marker planning systems have been in use for some years, providing markers for the cutting room more rapidly, more accurately and with more information. The sequence from initial design to marker planning is usually integrated, because one supplier provides all the equipment.

Sewing room

In the sewing room both the Unit Production System (UPS) and Modular Manufacturing (or sometimes the Toyota Sewing System after its inventors) offer appropriate means to achieve Quick Response. These are dealt with in more detail in Chapter 9.

2

Design and Innovation

The nature of design

Design, like civilisation, education, and management, is a word with many depths of meaning. Only philosophical method will strip off all the meanings to provide a coherent and comprehensive view. The reader should, however, be aware of the attitudes taken by the authors:

(1) The boundary between design and art is not always clear. The authors use design in the sense of creating products for profit. Art needs neither production nor profit. To carry this further and try to differentiate precisely between design and art runs the risk of arguing about words in ways unrelated to created objects, which is irrelevant to this book.

(2) Design is related to invention. The most convenient use of the term invention is to consider it as an important or original step in design, something more fundamental and less specific. Again there is no clear boundary. The invention of sleeves and trousers, the principle of bifurcation, is both ancient and undocumented. In modern times there have been, perhaps, only three clothing inventions: the bra began to separate from the corset in the 1880s and again in the 1920s; the self-supporting trouser, requiring neither belt nor braces, was invented in the 1930s; and tights, or panty-hose, were created in the 1960s when the mini-skirt made stockings impractical.

(3) The process of design begins with market research and continues by originating new styles, developing samples, refining business objectives and achieving commercial garments. Feedback from both manufacturing and the market place continues until the last garment in a style has been sold. This view of the design process is

valid in most manufacturing fields, but in many sectors of the clothing industry fashion design describes only the originating of new styles.

This restriction of the term to only one part of what other industries see as an integrated process of design can lead to some unfortunate results. In some cases it gives rise to a form of elitism which inhibits communication between design and manufacturing. Again the process of developing samples and refining business objectives may so dilute the original concept as to make the designer's contribution seem almost redundant. Since education usually reflects perceived social needs, and in this case commercial needs, the restriction of the idea of design to originating new styles produced two courses: the more highly regarded 'design' courses and those courses dealing with the remainder of the design process, a distinction now becoming less obvious at last.

(4)   The observed characteristics of designers commonly include strongly developed personalities, self-assurance, lack of conformity to received ideas and little need to be sociable and mix with others.

(5)   The essence of creativity is not the romantic notion of imagining something new, simply as if it were out of thin air, but resides in selecting the one thing out of many that might be used for a defined purpose. The essential process is one of choice. The effective designer can be recognised by the wide range of elements considered and the skill and judgement used to select and combine the elements of a new style: shapes, colours and textures. Design is visual thinking, perhaps of a higher order than verbal thinking. Visual thinking comprehends ideas in parallel rather than one after another: shapes, colours and textures as an integrated whole rather than separately.

(6)   This argument concludes therefore by asserting that designing is an arm of marketing. For a business to make a profit design must be market led, market driven and market justified.

Marketing

Marketing consists of identifying a need and satisfying it. One of the most famous examples is the creation of the British National Health Service in 1948. The cash nexus was not as simple as buying an article of clothing in a retail store, but both need and satisfaction were enormous.

Forty years on, identifying needs has become much more sophisticated, using concepts of market segmentation. In the past, companies identified and satisfied needs less by an organised approach through market research towards targeting a section of the market and more by employing common sense, flair and 'hunch'. In a less organised market these qualities had greater opportunities to achieve success. For many years the Spirella Company ran a highly profitable business offering a service to customers at home. It was morally acceptable because many women would have felt inhibited at undressing in a public place like a retail store. It satisfied a physical need because women's bodies, in the earlier years of the 20th century, were more variable, often more obese and were more in need of surgical support than they are today. It met a fashion need because the irregularities of body surface anatomy needed reshaping so that a woman was able to wear the often tighter fitting clothing of the times. It also met an economic need because a full corset of, say, the early 1930s was almost a capital purchase rather than a consumable, priced at three to four times the average weekly wage. Yet all these bases of the home fitted corset market have disappeared over the years.

In the 1950s a Swedish rainwear manufacturer marketed in a speculative way, at the top of its range, a proofed coat in 100 per cent silk fibre. Within a year demand outran its capability to supply, and continued for some years.

In the late 1930s the Simpson Company contemplated the prevailing fashion of Oxford 'bags' supported by belt or braces and predicted that many men, prepared to pay a higher price, wanted a straight trouser with a self-supporting waistband. The Daks trouser, worn both alone and as part of a suit (including with a dinner jacket) remains with us, and has been copied and adapted in many guises, although the belt as a fashion item has latterly restricted this.

Market segmentation

Modern ideas of market segmentation have been around since the 1950s. The concept influences a company to divide its markets into separate consumer targets. The power of the idea is that it provides an intellectual basis for the marketing drives of a company, in a situation of intense competition. It could be said that from the beginning clothing companies approached only a segment of the market by the range of garments they chose to manufacture or retail (men's, women's, children's); a social class by the prices charged; and a geographical area through a limited range of outlets.

What drives market segmentation is the desire of companies to develop specific approaches to specific segments of the market, where they perceive market needs are unsatisfied or only partially satisfied. Customers can now buy shorts for running, for hiking, for playing football or tennis, for swimming, for sleeping in or for lounging on the beach – not that the customer necessarily restricts their wearing to these activities. Indeed the cut of skin shorts for cycling has translated in lurex fabric to disco wear for young men and women.

Market segmentation divides the consumers in the total market into groups which are capable of being attracted to buy. There are many variables in a population of customers. Intelligence quotient, political orientation and manual dexterity are little regarded by marketing departments. In the marketing of clothing groups of customers are defined according to those who buy similar clothing.

Companies have specialised in supplying male or female clothing for generations. Offering garments for a specific age range has always been one marketing strategy, but has become more subtle as ever more age segments are defined. After the era of purely local retailing and manufacturing, some regional and national enterprises grew up which differentiated their ranges after experience rather than by planning, except for thinking of metropolitan and provincial or south and north.

Both manufacturing and retail businesses have always in one sense aimed their garments at separate income groups through the mechanism of pricing. The search for useful market segments nowadays, however, divides a population by income, social class, occupation and place in the family life cycle. High income alone is frequently a desirable indicator of a market segment, but more useful is the amount of income available after all household bills have been paid. This enabled companies to identify the segment aged between 15 and 25 years. Again, combining income with age throws up the newly affluent elderly, who may spend more conservatively on their own clothing but lavish money on more spectacular clothing for their grandchildren than the children's parents are likely to. Further factors may be ethnic grouping within Britain, and of course nationality in export markets.

Within and across all these groups are various types of behaviour among customers. Two types of general behaviour affecting the decision to purchase clothing are lifestyle (often characterised by words such as straight, status-seeker, fashion-follower) and personality (using scales of, for instance, gregariousness and ambition). Further types of behaviour relate more closely to the decision to buy clothing:

- whether the purchase is for regular use or a specific occasion;
- whether the buyer is a regular wearer, a first time buyer, a non-wearer (or an ex-wearer);
- how strong is the loyalty of the buyer to the retail outlet or the manufacturer on a scale from none to absolute loyalty;
- how ready is the buyer to buy – ignorant of the range, just aware of it, knowledgeable, interested or intending to buy;
- what benefits the buyer seeks from the purchase – prestige,

economy, comfort or the urge to satisfy a particular clothing need
such as sportswear;
● how responsive the buyer is to the various factors in the marketing
mix – sales promotion and advertising, service, price and quality.

A further type of segmentation stems from the use to which the
wearer puts the clothing. The most obvious categories here are the
many sports requiring specialised clothing: mountaineering and sailing,
swimming, running and jogging, golf and cricket, snooker and others.
Motoring in its beginnings used to demand special garments; cycling at
first spawned the Norfolk jacket but latterly has turned to skin shorts.
Photography promotes individual clothing. Again stage costumes have
their own market. In addition the number of occupations requiring a
uniform grows, not only the traditional and formal military types but
public service occupations of all kinds: airlines, public utilities, local
authority services and even, lately, junior bank staff.

Market research

One identifiable segment is maternity wear, which serves as a good
example of the research needed before going into a market. Maternity
wear is often sold by mail order but also through high street shops. To
avoid the traditional floral smock the customer has to discover local
shops, if they are available, or use higher priced boutiques towards the
top end of the market; a choice between style and price. If a company
wished to enter this niche in the market, it would have to carry out
research to establish the segment it was targeting. The Central
Statistical Office annual abstract of statistics shows the age distribution
of the female population, and live births by age of mother in the UK
for a series of years. From these statistics trends can be identified for
the age of mother at the first birth and the variations for each age
group. It is necessary to add to this the expenditure on clothing by
women and the percentage of women in each age group who are
employed. Further it is necessary to discover by questionnaire what
percentage of pregnant women are likely to work until late in their
pregnancy and take maternity leave rather than leave employment; this
signifies a need for smart working clothes at a reasonable price. Finally
it is necessary to know the factors considered important in maternity
wear: such as comfort, price, style, size flexibility, fabric and so on.
Identifying a target segment by market research leads to developing a
marketing mix, which includes such factors as advertising and
promotion, the choice and design of retail outlets and of course the
design of a range of garments. Companies have created a series of retail
chains, differentiated by age, gender, lifestyle and buyer behaviour. In

short, managing design also means designing companies to market clothing.

Clothing and the body

The clothing people wear needs, in different situations, to keep their bodies warm or cool, to keep out wind or water, and always to permit the evaporation of perspiration from the surface of the body. These needs relate intimately to each other.

Keeping warm depends on the insulating power of still air. There is a layer of approximately three millimetres of air next to every surface, which is relatively resistant to movement. Thus an efficient insulator would contain within its structure many surfaces for air to cling to or pockets for air to lie in. In order to create a larger amount of still air a designer could vary the type of fibre, the structure of the fabric, the finish of the fabric and the way garments are constructed from fabrics. Although woollen structures – made up of crimped fibres with a scaly outer surface and hairy yarns resulting from fibres of different length – are traditionally the warmest, a sweater knitted from yarns of texturised acrylic fibre has more insulation than a jacket made from tightly woven worsted. Wool will absorb moisture and feel dry next to the skin. It then releases water to the environment very slowly and prevents sudden chilling.

Keeping out wind is important because wind displaces still air and destroys insulation. The principle of the 'windbreaker' is a closely woven synthetic fibre layer which protects the air spaces in the clothing underneath and maintains the boundary layer of air next to the body. Keeping out water is commonly achieved by water resistant fabric such as silicone-proofed cotton. These fabrics are not claimed to be waterproof.

Waterproofing woven fabrics by filling the spaces between the fibres with a coating provides proof against both wind and water. Unfortunately proofed fabrics do not let water or water vapour out, and perspiration builds up to make the garment wet on the inside.

The ease with which a fabric allows the passage of water vapour (its breathability) depends on the fibre, the weave and the thickness. With natural fibres weave and thickness do not affect this resistance, because water vapour passes through the fibres. With synthetic fibres the water vapour must travel along the surface of the fibres; hence the fabrics must be thin and of open weave. This does not provide much insulation.

The latest solution to this problem is a waterproof fabric with micropores – pores too small to let water pass in but able to let water vapour and air out. This is made from a thin sheet of PTFE (polytetrafluorethylene) expanded by stretching and annealing. This results in a membrane of a web of PTFE nodules connected by fine fibrils. The pores of the web are usually less than one micrometre in diameter, compared to molecules of water in water vapour at 0.0004 micrometres and the smallest droplets of water at more than 100 micrometres. The membrane is bonded to a range of different fabrics and the outside is protected by coating the membrane with a hydrophilic polymer. This is a polymer where the fibres have been given a surface treatment which helps the water in the water vapour to spread along the surfaces.

Two other factors affect keeping warm. Fibres parallel to the direction of heat flow conduct heat more efficiently to the wearer's environment. A prime example is velvet; crushed velvet insulates more efficiently than velvet pile. Colour affects heat flow: white reflects and black absorbs heat, but this property is affected by the surface texture of the fabric.

Integrating this information about fibre and fabric properties with garment structures suggests four ways in which designers can provide the means to keep warm. The first is to construct garments of thick fabrics or with quilted, down-filled areas; or to assemble outfits consisting of several layers, each with its air space. The second is to keep the torso and head well insulated so that the body can supply heat to the hands and feet. The third is to protect the insulating layers from wind and water while maintaining 'breathability', in the ways outlined above. The fourth is to provide ventilation so that water vapour can be dissipated and sweating avoided. This can be achieved by 'chimney' effects at neck and waist and large enough openings at cuff and trouser bottoms.

Similarly designers may provide ways to keep cool: thin garments of fabrics which allow the passage of water vapour, garments which block the sun's heat (which may be white and thicker) and loose clothing which allows a free circulation of air around the body. In addition, the designer should use materials which inhibit moisture from lying on the surface of the skin. One solution to this is a layer of cotton over a synthetic layer because cotton has the effect of drawing moisture through the synthetic.

These considerations affect designers' choices when designing military clothing, much sporting clothing and outdoor clothing, especially that which must perform effectively in extremes of climate; but a conventional range of fabrics and garment structures suffices for many garments worn in centrally heated atmospheres and temperate climates. For these human physiology is not at the forefront of the designer's mind.

Recently, retailers in Scotland have reported that one model of a well-known make of mountaineering jacket has achieved cult status at an Edinburgh disco. It might be very difficult to unravel the causes of this phenomenon so that designers could reproduce it.

Social psychology of clothing

The design of clothing primarily influences the decision to buy; but one step behind the decision to buy is the behaviour of people towards clothing. From an early age children want to conform to the latest fashion, be it Mickey Mouse or turtles. The proportion of fashion innovators in the population will probably always be small, the proportion of active followers of fashion large, and the proportion of ignorers of fashion a smaller group drawn from the traditionalists, the old and the poor. It is easy to forget that approximately 5 per cent of clothing turnover is through market stalls, where the influences of fashion are later and less various; and an unknown percentage is secondhand clothing through charity shops and jumble sales. It is always a surprise to learn that the organisation with the largest number of retail clothing outlets is the charity Oxfam, although they have by no means the largest turnover.

Income

Hence one large factor which determines the behaviour of people towards clothing is the amount of their income available to buy clothing. It may be oversimplifying to state that the newer and higher the fashion, the more expensive it is likely to be; but it must be remembered that fashion often expresses not only innovation but status. Even the most well-known example of fashion emanating from 'the streets' – the teddy boy image of the 1950s – was for the buyer a major investment, based on the large free incomes of young men in continuous employment living at home.

Lifestyle

Assuming sufficient income to exercise choice, people wear clothing to suit their lifestyle. Lifestyle has many meanings, some of which are very general while others differentiate groups.

Slimmer shape

One important component of lifestyle over the last generation has been the movement to standardise the human body to a slimmer shape by dieting and exercise. Two generations ago obesity was much more common among both men and women and was socially acceptable. In that climate there was a proliferation of chains of menswear retailers offering made-to-measure suits, corset makers offering a home service to individual customers, and home dressmaking or 'private dressmakers' serving individuals from their homes. Technologically speaking, the height of men's pattern cutting expertise was the drafting of accurate patterns for corpulent figures.

Since the 1940s the made-to-measure market in all its aspects has declined continuously, partly because of the social desire for slimmer and hence more standardised body shapes, but also because made-to-measure garments are inherently more expensive to produce and because pattern cutting and sizing based on statistically sound sizing surveys are more effective. Nowadays the made-to-measure market is limited to very highly priced garments, to the relatively few with disproportionate figures, and to those whose job requires they wear clothes with a perfect fit, perhaps including commissionaires, military officers and airline pilots.

Simpler clothing

Another component of lifestyle is the demand for simpler clothing, which reflects both active working lives and emancipation. The most obvious evidence of this is the wearing of fewer items in an outfit; fewer petticoats, fewer vests, fewer waistcoats, fewer hats, and the demise of the liberty bodice. In addition the size and coverage of individual items has reduced; jackets, if worn, instead of frock coats, shorter skirts, shorter shorts (apart from American Bermudas), more exiguous swimwear, and briefs instead of directoire knickers. Furthermore, people require that clothing be simpler to doff and don, with zips and press studs instead of buttons and buttonholes, more frequent use of elastication, slip-on shoes, coat shirts with attached collars, more self-supporting trousers and belts with fewer braces, tights avoiding the need for suspender belts, bra-slips and Y-fronts.

Finally, people demand clothing that is simpler to maintain, preferably by washing or otherwise by standard dry cleaning techniques. One exception which customers tolerate is a sheepskin coat. This attracts the higher maintenance costs of specialised dry cleaning which people are prepared to meet only because a sheepskin coat is considered to be a long-term investment. In relation to washing, the design of clothing forms part of an after-care system which includes the design of washing cycles in machines, the chemistry of detergents, methods of drying and the attempt to eliminate or reduce the time-consuming activity of ironing.

A striking exception to this general demand for simpler clothing is the wedding dress, which requires more undergarments, is full in length, is relatively difficult to put on and is not normally washed or dry cleaned. The minority who hire a wedding dress benefit from paying about half the price for an equivalent garment, and the dress is usually hired three times before it is scrapped. Customers in the USA show different consumer behaviour towards another example of what might be termed one-wear garments. Graduation gowns are manufactured from disposable fabrics which give good performance for one day at an acceptably low price. Translating this concept to wedding dresses will be very much more difficult in spite of the potential economic advantages, because the achievement of the right wedding dress image from disposable fabrics is much more unlikely. In any case the traditional demands of a wedding are reflected in a type of clothing whose costs people are willing to bear.

Fashion

It is the complex of activities and attitudes called fashion which influences the behaviour of different groups in relation to clothing. Polhemus in his book *Fashion and Anti-Fashion* makes an important distinction: those in society who wear traditional, classic, relatively unchanging styles use clothing as symbols of continuity or changelessness, while those who wear the latest fashions use clothing as symbols of change and progress. Polhemus contrasts the use of tartan in kilts, traditional since the late nineteenth century, with the fashionable uses of tartan in skirts or almost any other garment.

Rouse, in *Understanding Fashion*, after a sound and comprehensive history of fashion writing, identifies fashionable behaviour as different from taste and as a sort of conspicuous consumption, implying some leisure time to pursue it, as being up-to-date, as seeking some sort of prestige, and as being creative in some sense by selecting the styles which will be emulated. Of course, fashion is not as hierarchical as in the past when it was handed down from Paris, but fashion ideas are selected and promoted among groups in society at all levels. Hence a number of looks are developed which appeal to different groups.

The design system

In the early 1930s J. Livingston Lowes wrote *The Road to Xanadu* in which, using diary references, he related the content of Coleridge's poem *The Rime of the Ancient Mariner* to Coleridge's reading matter while he was writing the poem. Lowes showed that almost every phrase in the poem embodied what the poet had been reading. Yet Coleridge was not a plagiarist, because he had so selected and transformed his material as to produce a new piece of imaginative writing. The output of a fashion designer comes from a similar process.

The most creative fashion designers have available for selection elements from the whole history of fashion and costume throughout the world, for study and reflection the origin of all the current styles and 'looks', and for inspiration modern social trends in painting, film, architecture and television. Although working separately and secretly (copyright on original designs is an active issue), designers often produce collections with common underlying themes.

The majority of designers who cater for a large output, work as part of a marketing system which acts as a pluralist decision-making process. The elements in this process comprise:

(1) Well-known international designers who originate themes or trends which others may follow;
(2) All types of media who report and predict the shapes, colours and textures which make up the matrix of fashion;
(3) Retail buyers who seek to select styles for their segment of the market;
(4) Individual customers who make decisions to buy.

All the elements in the system communicate through fashion shows and consultancies, by printed words and illustrations and by watching shop windows.

The practice of design

The first phase of design is a brief which defines the garment type, age group, purpose, climate and price range which the designer should aim at. The later stages of the design process may lead to adaptation of the design brief.

The second phase is research. The designer must of course be immersed in all the current means of communication of fashion ideas. The designer may also look for new ideas in historic costume, garments from many cultures, the forms of architecture, the dramatisation of fashion in the performing arts, and the colours, textures and shapes of plants and animals. Even political events have their spin-off; at the time of writing surplus East German military uniforms are being promoted as a fashion item. New fabrics, colours or trims may provide inspiration. The company's purchase of a machine, such as a pin-tucking machine, may stimulate a designer to design for it in a way that is not simply a desire to make full use of an expensive asset.

In the third phase, the designer's collection may begin with the selection of fabrics or the development of a theme through a series of sketches of front and back views. This is extended into a story board, as large as necessary, to display related colours, textures, trims and

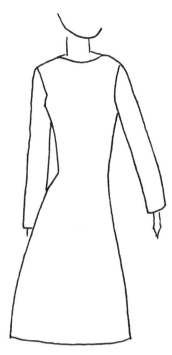

Fig. 2.1 An overall silhouhette.

sketches which build up to a theme or story to be used within the company and with customers.

Fourthly, the working drawing or sketch is a diagram in proportion to the body of a style selected for development as a product. It should include all the information necessary to produce a pattern and a sample: seams, darts, detailed style features, samples of fabrics and trims.

The shapes the designer selects to represent concepts are infinitely varied. The overall silhouette is the outline (Fig. 2.1). Within the silhouette the designer creates lines, or seams, which define panels. The seams may be plain or the lines emphasised by single or double topstitching. The seams may represent vertical, horizontal, diagonal or curved lines. The lines may create symmetry or asymmetry between different parts of a garment. Again the designer is concerned with proportion or the relationship between each part and the whole garment, for instance that between bodice and skirt.

The designer also includes decisions about sleeve length and shape, cuffs, collar shape and type, yokes, pockets (patch, inset or those in a seam), design details such as belts and epaulettes, fastenings, braids and other trims, fabric treatments such as fringes, gathers, pleats, tucks, smocking, shirring and quilting, the use of contrasting fabrics and surface decoration such as embroidery (Fig. 2.2).

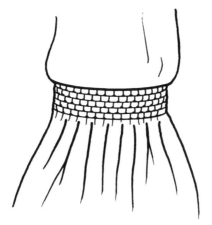

Fig. 2.2   Surface decoration: waist shirring.

This summary of the shapes with which the designer wrestles to create the initial concept of a style is intended to give only an impression of what starts the total process of design. There are many books which provide examples of the shapes available.

Computer aided design (CAD)

CAD for textiles is highly developed. It can simulate fibre thicknesses, colour blends, different twist levels of yarn and the surface effects of brushing and slubs. Fabric constructions can be simulated and printed out with great accuracy. These design effects can be linked to manufacturing cost and, in the case of knitting, to the driving of machinery. For CAD garments, simulations require a larger number and much more complex programs. There are still severe limitations on the translations of three dimensional designs into two dimensional patterns. For garments CAD has three stages: the actual design of colour, texture and silhouette, the realisation in patterns, and the interface with marker making and cutting.

CAD systems can produce designs in a number of ways. The first is to design from scratch using a tablet and stylus, with colours and textures from large 'libraries' used to provide an initial simulation. Again previous designs are recalled and modified. Further, it is possible to produce an image from photographs, which are digitised and can be modified using different drapes and lighting. All these can produce high resolution colour prints.

One system builds a three dimensional image on which fabric can be laid, the model rotated, and both lighting and drape adjusted. Parts of the garment can be removed and the shape changed before returning it to the screen. This system can print out a pattern for a sample or for a pattern cutter to adjust. In the case of very simple garments it is possible to go straight to the marker. Standard blocks may be modified to provide silhouettes with only minor input from a pattern cutter. The biggest difficulties arise with radical design changes, where the system has no basis to build on.

The achievement of shape

Patterns aim to interpret the design and represent the component parts of the garment. Four conditions are necessary to achieve success:

(1) Patterns should reproduce the fashion image and proportions of the designer's sketch;
(2) Patterns should reflect the details of body surface anatomy;
(3) Patterns should take account of fabric reactions during the manufacturing process;
(4) Patterns should conform with the body measurements of a particular size.

The methods of achieving (1), (2) and (3) are generally flat pattern cutting, modelling (or draping) and copying.

Flat pattern cutting

Flat pattern cutting translates the proportions of the designer's working sketch into a series of pattern components which, in a finished garment, will fit the figure for which the prototype pattern is designed. The pattern cutter usually begins from a block pattern, designed to be used over a range of styles and sizes. The cutter adjusts edges and seam lines to accommodate style features, and changes the position and number of darts and seams.

This simple statement, of course, covers a multitude of subtle techniques which it is not the purpose of this book to describe. These techniques marry mathematical and creative approaches. Among pattern cutters there has from time to time been tension between proponents of the two approaches, but commercial success requires a proper integration of both. In the creation of a prototype pattern the creative approach dominates the process, but as the development of a pattern proceeds through production the mathematical element becomes more important.

Block patterns (or basic patterns) are constructed according to the measurements of the base size with the addition of curved lines for armholes, forks and sleeveheads. Since pattern cutting is empirical, block patterns are normally tested and revised until they are seen to be consistently useful. The range of styles a pattern cutter may develop from one basic block will of course vary from one company to another, but radically different shapes usually need a different block. For instance, the pattern cutter will derive a different block for trousers although it is related to the skirt block. It is often convenient to prepare a block for looser fitting trousers (with pleats, waist fullness or flared legs). Special kimono and raglan blocks will be prepared from, and related to, the basic bodice and sleeve blocks. Blocks in relation to the size scale, however, are another matter. One block will normally cover a short size scale, such as 10, 12, 14, 16. However, for a much more extended size scale reaching into the 20s, or for the usually long size scales in some menswear, more blocks may be introduced when the pattern cutter feels that the increasing size changes the proportions of different parts of the figure.

Modelling

Modelling plays an important part in draped designs, using loosely hanging folds, swathes, festoons and graduated folds. Many pattern cutters prefer to model these designs wholly on the stand or figure. This may be the quickest way to develop a new idea, accurately achieve a new effect or test the draping qualities of a new fabric.

Copying

Copying is self explanatory. The pattern cutter buys a garment, takes it to pieces (usually) and uses the components to cut a set of patterns. This ensures a quick result but dangers lie in the distortion of fabric during manufacture and in whether the pattern cutter can relate the resulting patterns to the company's basic blocks.

The prototype pattern, by whatever means achieved, is used to cut the first samples. On acceptance for production, the pattern cutter adds seam allowances, turnups, notches and grain lines, plus the regular means of identifying style and size.

Fabric reactions

Taking account of fabric reactions relates to shrinking and stretching. Clearly, a consistent amount of warp shrinkage can be offset by lengthening patterns. For garments made wholly or partly from stretch fabrics pattern cutters construct patterns which allow for the amount of extension required in the finished garment. The success of this procedure depends on wearer trials and a monitoring of the consistency of fabric supplies. Tailored garments are a special case. The manufacture and pressing of toilored garments include a significant amount of localised shaping by shrinking and stretching. The enhancement of the shape contained in the patterns is mainly obtained in wool and wool-rich garments. The chief areas where this sort of moulding takes place are around the end of darts and on collars, shoulders, sleeveheads and sometimes trouser legs. The bust and waist of a tailored jacket, originally created by the pattern's seams and darts, can be accentuated by pressing on shaped presses. (The International Association of Clothing Designers, a menswear group in the USA, used to approve the new season's shape of these presses at their conventions.)

Grading

Grading patterns achieves conformity for a group of people within a certain size. Made-to-measure garments are made for customers whose measurements are known beforehand. Ready-to-wear garments are made for customers whom the manufacturer predicts will fall within a certain size coding, which represents given measurements.

The manufacturer usually bases these predictions on a series of anthropometrical surveys of women, carried out on a national scale between the 1940s and 1960s in the USA, Britain, West Germany and France. Collectively, the surveys covered 60 different body measurements. Statistical analysis of the data led to decisions about which were key measurements (e.g. hips, bust) to which others could be related, and the groups into which the population could be divided by creating standard intervals between the key measurements. This led to the creation of size charts with each size identified by a symbol or code (e.g. 12, 14, 16 in Britain), with a 4 cm interval between sizes up to size 14 and a 5 cm interval above that (see British Standard 3666: 1982). Each national size scale follows the same general pattern, but different decisions have been taken about size intervals and, for instance, the drops between hip and bust.

The manufacturer selects the part of the national size scale which covers his particular market. Even within this market it would be economically impossible to produce garments for every variation in the size range. Hence the most practical system is that which fits the largest number of women using the fewest sizes. In practice actual garment sizes differ slightly owing to manufacturing inaccuracies. Nor does the British Standard specify one set of measurements for each size symbol, but a narrow range (4 cm for both hip and bust). So the measurements individual manufacturers use against the size symbols also vary. Most garments have an ease allowance in addition to the net body measurement. For all these reasons actual sizes for apparently similar garments are not always identical. Customers are well aware of this

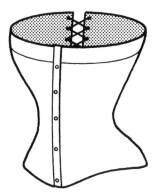

Fig. 2.3   Corset about 1905.

and are willing to shop around and find the retail store or manufacturer whose garments best fit their individual figures.

Grading is the method by which the pattern cutter creates patterns for a whole range of sizes from the agreed base size. For instance, the total difference in girth between British sizes is 4 or 5 cm. It is the task of grading to proportion those increments among the different parts or panels of the garment according to detailed, logical rules. Since this is the more mathematical end of the pattern cutting sequence, it is no surprise to find that grading was the first pattern cutting operation to be computerised in the mid-1960s.

Case study

The history of corsetry in the 20th century illustrates how many of the themes and influences so far outlined come together to produce garment designs offered to the market.

Around 1905 corsets were made of heavy cotton and stiffened by whaleboning, with lace-up backs (Fig. 2.3). Their shape unnaturally suppressed women's waists into the small size decreed by the fashion of the time. A more expensive corset in cream figured silk, with lace and ribbons and suspenders, was also available, with elaborate shaping including gussets to smooth curves to bust and hips. By 1910 corsets were longer and straighter. Corsetry relied on inelastic fabrics reinforced by boning to shape the figure. Elastication could be used only in small gussets or panels, because the rubber used was coarse and available only in short pieces. With fashion emphasising the waist, women bought corsets according to the waist measurement they could achieve.

The market perceived the First World War as imposing practicality and functionalism on clothing. The emancipated woman of the 1920s

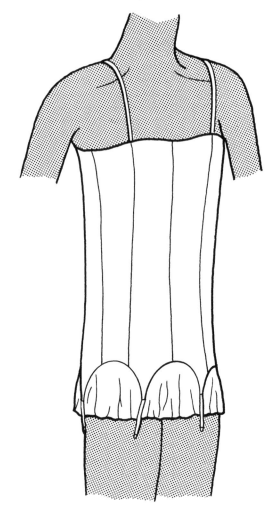

Fig. 2.4 Corselette of 1925.

rejected corsets which constricted the waist in favour of simpler garments which flattened the figure to meet the fashionable needs of the tube line, the extreme opposite of the 1905 woman. By 1925 the corselette in mercerised cotton with side panels of elastic used only a little boning over the stomach to give limited control (Fig. 2.4).

By about 1930, rubber could be imported in an uncoagulated form and then extruded as 'Lastex' threads, which were fine enough to be woven or knitted into two-way stretch fabrics. The 'roll-on' girdle of 1932 (Fig. 2.5), produced on a circular knitting machine, allowed figure control without a rigid construction. These developments of machine and fabric encouraged the designers of the time to create more feminine fashions, with curves reappearing after the tube line and

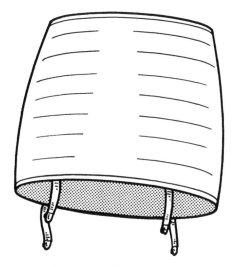

Fig. 2.5   Roll-on girdle 1932.

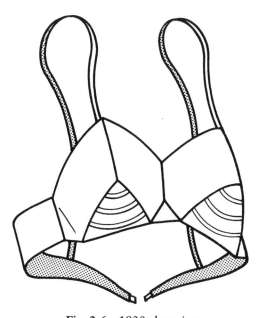

Fig. 2.6   1930s brassiere.

making corsetry much more comfortable. Less distortion of the figure also went along with the fashionable wearing of soft jersey and bias cut outer garments. Manufacturers now produced former non-stretch fabrics in elasticated form – Lastex baptiste and satin Lastex, and later elastic nets and 'power lace'.

By the late 1920s the brassiere, with definite cup shaping, was often

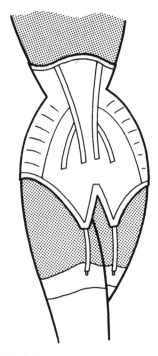

Fig. 2.7 'New Look' corset.

separate from a hip-shaping girdle. In 1935 the Warner Company realised that, in addition to the overall bust measurement, it was necessary to incorporate the size of the breast itself into brassiere design, and developed cup fittings A, B, C and D, the basis of modern cup fitting systems, although they were not in general use for some years. To design a brassiere which accommodated natural figure shape, designers began to use darted cups, seams and circular stitching. In addition, undercup wiring, stiffening and padding all began in the 1930s (Fig. 2.6).

Interestingly, for a few years after 1947, the 'new look' required a more tightly suppressed waist. This was the last time the body was forcefully shaped by corsetry. Fig. 2.7 shows a high fashion 'Waspie' girdle of the time, made of heavy satin with padded hips and back lacing.

After 1945 the use of nylon in corsetry fabrics became widespread. Its first advantage was its tensile strength and resistance to abrasion, allowing the use of lighter weight fabrics. By the late 1940s fabrics such as taffeta and voile had replaced the heavy cottons and satins, and nylon elastic net was used in stretch panels. Secondly, it simplified washing with no danger of shrinkage, and allowed rapid drying owing to its low moisture absorption. The third advantage was the low price of nylon fibre and fabrics in comparison with those previously

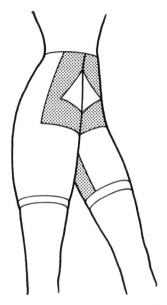

Fig. 2.8 1960s panti-girdle.

available. In 1931 a corselette might have cost eight guineas (£8.40p), more than twice the average weekly wage and therefore a considerable investment. Developments in warp knitting in the early 1950s meant that long runs of two-way stretch fabrics could be produced. In the mid-1950s designers created the all elastic corselette, the first being the well-known Little X by Silhouette.

Even with the use of nylon, corsetry in the 1950s was still comparatively substantial. In the early 1960s designers began to use fabrics containing elastane (formerly called elastomeric) fibre. One common brand name is Lycra. This began a period of very lightweight control and simplified construction. Soft, supple stretch fabrics could be dyed and printed, with scope for lace constructions. Fabrics with elastane satisfied the demand for light, natural foundationwear which accompanied the outerwear fashions started by the mini-skirt of the late 1960s. Designers produced the panti-girdle (Fig. 2.8), panti-corselette and stretch control brief. The desire to achieve natural shape led to the 'see-through' and 'no-bra' look. Foundation garments made of hosiery type fabrics, with very little trimming, followed the body contours like a second skin.

Elastane has great tensile strength and very good powers of recovery. This means that fabrics can be sheerer and lighter but give the same control as the heavier Lastex fabrics. Elastane has better resistance to abrasion, perspiration and lotions, and will keep its whiteness, in its natural state, when washed. It can also be dyed, with a high degree of colour fastness. The percentage of elastane in a fabric generally varies between 15 per cent and 40 per cent, according to the amount of control and shape retention expected. For example, a lightweight panti-corselette, made using three dimensional knitting with pouch shaping to accommodate bust and seat prominences, might include 19 per cent of 40 denier elastane.

Stretch, pull-on garments require only very simple fastenings, if any. Garments with elastane can control natural figure shape without stress. In many corselettes, designers incorporate panels giving firmer control, using higher denier elastane or higher elastane content, perhaps over the stomach or seat area. Elastane fabrics can be designed for specific uses, from body stockings to high control girdles. Designers are able to achieve specific objectives of control, shaping, uplift and support as well as aesthetic qualities in garments which are often intended to be seen through outer garments.

Sales of bras have been maintained or increased. Indeed the invention of moulding in the 1970s provided an extension to the range, with a very soft, simple construction using a high stretch fabric of elastane and nylon. Moulded bras represent a significant proportion of the total number manufactured, but this could decline if fashion were to demand a firmer, more structured look.

However, decline in corset sales has continued. This began first with the wearing of tights, because many women wore a girdle purely as something to hang their stockings on. With more casual styles of both life and dress, and with diet and exercise producing slimmer figures, the demand for corsetry continues to diminish. A Du Pont survey in the USA discovered that many women saw buying a girdle as a depressing admission of defeat. Thus while there is a steady market for the minority who desire control of shape through corsetry, the majority of women for the majority of the time (except for perhaps a few formal occasions) reject even the lightest of foundations below the waist.

The story of foundation wear in the 20th century illustrates the interactions of fashion, lifestyle, fibre, fabric and construction methods in the process of fashion design and product development.

3

Management of the Process of Design and Product Development

The process of design and product development is, as has been seen, very complex. It consists of a number of stages, all of which are influenced by a variety of aesthetic, technological and financial factors.

The first stage is essentially innovative: ideas are generated and the design concept results from market research. This market research may be fundamental or it may be no more than a reaction to existing sales figures (or somebody else's). The idea is then developed by the production of a prototype pattern and the making of samples. At this stage decisions may be made based on estimates of sales and certainly estimates of costs. With a favourable reaction, the product will be appraised for production and the patterns adapted for production requirements. The production patterns are then graded, which leads to the making of markers and the final specifications. The whole development will then be handed over to the manufacturing department from which there will be a feedback which may lead to further modifications. The ultimate test will be the reaction from the market place and the feedback from it.

The whole operation requires management, since management provides control but also stimulus. Management must be able to motivate, provide leadership and account for the different psychologies of the groups of people who are likely to be involved in the process, ranging from the creative designers to the different approach of those in production and financial control. The term 'design management' is one that frequently occurs in the management vocabulary. It means variously the management of designers and management by designers. To this confusion in terminology must also be added the one well-known in the clothing industry where design traditionally means only the idea generation of a style, instead of the more broad ranging definition where design is the whole process of innovation and product development up to the point where the product goes into production. Thus in many parts of the clothing industry the designer simply produces style ideas, perhaps sketches with a sample of fabric; and a pattern cutter then takes on the development process. The essence of the problem, however, is that success is based on efficient integration of the whole process in such a way that creativity is not stifled but becomes a means to an end, not an end in itself. For without successful production capability, technological and quality control and realistic costing, the whole enterprise will end in failure. This is the ultimate test of management.

In a sense all people with a line controlling function are managers, irrespective of the discipline in which they began their career. Although managing directors may have begun life as a designer, pattern cutter or laboratory technician, in their role as managing directors they must integrate and balance the various claims and counterclaims of the whole operation and must not allow their initial training to influence them overtly in any particular direction. Similarly, individual middle managers, whether their basic discipline be design or production, would not function to the best advantage of the organisation if they operated as if their part of the enterprise was the most important part, to the detriment of all others. The reality is that such homogeneity is difficult to achieve and hence organisations develop a variety of management structures in order to try and achieve what in essence may be impossible.

Growth of a business

The problem may be illustrated by tracing the development of a typical clothing operation. Traditionally, it starts as a one person business or at least as a small family business with one person very much in charge. That person will do virtually everything, starting with market research: i.e. finding a niche which a small firm can exploit, maybe by supplying a particular customer. That person will certainly come up with styles and will produce the patterns and carry out all the buying of fabric and trimmings, in order to start the production process. In all probability they will employ machinists, maybe their own family, although inevitably they will have to train them. They will certainly do the selling, i.e. the contact with the major customers. There is in fact

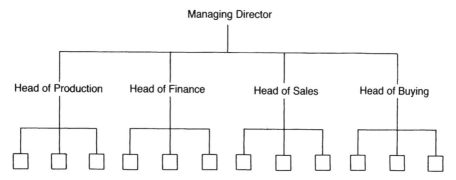

Fig. 3.1 Typical 'family tree' organisation (higher levels only).

no management organisation; one person alone is the manager with no delegation apart from instructions passed on to machinists. In some operations the work may be done on a CMT (cut, make and trim) basis, so that the owner/manager may have to produce specifications for outside contractors to work to.

As the business expands and more people are employed, there will come a point when delegation takes place. A designer or a production manager could be employed, but one of the earliest additions is likely to be financial assistance. Many businesses in the clothing area start because someone has a fashion concept and identifies a particular market; their skill is not in financial control and if they do not acquire that skill either for themselves or by employing someone, the business is likely to flounder. Even so, the management structure is that of the wheel, with the owner/manager as the hub and all sub-managers operating through that hub. No decision is taken without the owner/manager's consent, and the structure is the spokes of the wheel without any rim. There is very little contact in decision-making terms between the sub-managers.

Further growth in the organisation, however, inevitably means that the sub-managers begin to acquire hierarchies of their own, and it is not long before the manager at the centre cannot physically control all parts of the organisation or be in contact with it. Decisions have to be made between sub-managers. At that point the organisation takes on a typical hierarchical structure, or family tree organisation (Fig. 3.1). All sub-managers may now even be directors, operating through the senior manager or managing director, but they do have contact with each other.

Usually in a clothing firm there will be a production director and a financial director, but after that the situation begins to vary. Traditionally there is likely to be a sales director with a sales force for contacting customers. Where is design in this organisation?

In many companies serving the retail sector with a standard product range such as men's shirts, where fashion does not dictate great changes and where the retention of a traditional image is the company's marketing angle, the designers could well find themselves acting as pattern cutters, making minor modifications to standard patterns. Probably located in the production department, they are called on to make alterations at the direction of the managing director, or even the sales director who might at this point be called the merchandise director even though the sales force are responsible to him. Such a system was typical of much of the clothing industry, even in women's fashions, up until the 1980s.

In effect the creative ideas of these organisations, which were often a result of copying, directly or indirectly, originals created by international designers, came from the managing director. Growing realisation, however, that fashion and design were essential to retain position in a competitive market has forced alterations on this hierarchical structure. The first step is generally to separate the design function, perhaps with the appointment of a design director, with a whole team of designers, generally stylists, operating as another part of the family tree hierarchy. In some cases design is seen as a function of marketing, so that a marketing director will be appointed with then perhaps a senior or head designer responsible to him. There will be a clear separation from either production or selling, although in many organisations the influence of the managing director in this area remains strong (unless the managing director has a particular financial control or orientation).

Alternative structures

The well known difficulty of the hierarchical structure is that it tends to develop 'empires', that is departments or divisions which are power-cultures in management terms and which are often more concerned to protect their own interests than to integrate for the benefit of the whole organisation. The organisation therefore functions through a series of confrontations between the various directors, and the orientation of the organisation depends on the strength of personality of those individuals, or perhaps on the bias of the area from which the Managing Director himself originated. Thus companies become production dominated, sales dominated or design dominated, with inevitably disastrous results. Decisions are not taken in the interests of the organisation as a whole but to protect part of the hierarchy. Therefore the influence of one part of the hierarchy becomes too high to the detriment of the other parts, reducing the overall viability of the product.

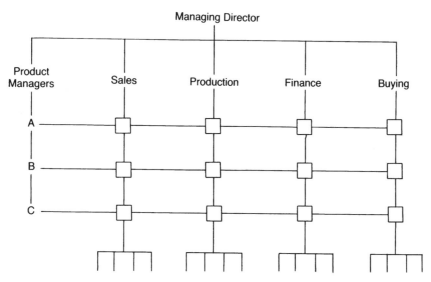

Fig. 3.2 Organisation chart showing a matrix type structure.

Typical results are that design innovation is stifled because the production department argues that it cannot cope with the variations of style required, or quality suffers because the design department insists on particular suppliers of fabric and trimmings which do not meet the performance of the company's section of the market. Many organisations in the 1980s, who quite correctly became design orientated and were successful, subsequently became victims of that success. Faced with an enormous sales increase and under enormous pressure from the sales department to increase production, they moved outside their own production capability to use other companies' manufacturing facilities. They did not have an organisation capable of controlling that outside production and so flooded the market with products of inferior quality, thus ultimately ruining their reputations.

The problem of the deficiencies of the hierarchical structure has occupied management theorists for some time, not only in relation to the clothing industry. A common approach has been the setting up of a matrix system. This indicates the roles of individuals and groups in various activities. The matrix is an arrangement of rows and columns. In the rows the activities are shown with broad functional responsibilities and authorities and the columns show the staff designations, such as sales, production, finance, etc. The person at an intersection of a row and a column has a role in an activity (Fig. 3.2).

Where an organisation has developed and may be producing and selling a wide product range, the organisation is seen in marketing terms, where products or designs are sold to meet individual markets.

Thus the products are divided into groups, each with a product manager or merchandise manager. A typical operation in womenswear might include product managers for blouses, skirts, trousers, etc. The product manager therefore has responsibility for all aspects of the product range in that designated area, and will link up in the matrix with design, production, finance or indeed with any other departmental function as appropriate. It is the product manager therefore who provides the integration by cutting across the boundaries in the hierarchical structure. The matrix is therefore a recipe for dynamic action. It can, however, become a recipe for dynamic confrontation.

The greatest difficulties are likely to be confrontation between product managers and production. This inevitably occurs over priorities in delivery and cost. As product managers seek to introduce variety into their ranges, so the costs of production rise; product managers may find that the costs they are incurring from their own production units are greater than those their competitors are incurring. Pressure therefore grows from those product managers to take their production requirements outside the organisation. This could be in the United Kingdom but more often is overseas. Matrix structures based around product centres may prove to be recipes for dynamic action; they may also lead to fundamental changes in the whole organisation.

The second source of problems in the product manager concept is likely to be in the relationship between the product manager and the design department. The need of the product manager to develop a range may conflict with the priorities of the design department outside their direct control. Yet in an operation which depends on fashion and innovation, it is essential that the innovation stage works correctly and efficiently. It is for this reason that some organisations have moved towards the product cell concept.

In this the design department as such disappears. Instead, each product manager operates a product cell in which innovation and ideas come from a designer and a fashion co-ordinator, although the latter may be employed across the whole company (Fig. 3.3). This cell concept is very much akin to the 'think tank' concept, where ideas are developed in an atmosphere of permanent confrontation between individuals, and then materialise to be developed in the design and product development chain. For many companies, both the designer and the fashion co-ordinator in the product cell may be outside consultants.

The idea of consultancy for any part of an organisation is not new. Developing organisations often find it more useful to take outside advice rather than employ their own personnel, at least initially, until they have developed a structure which best suits their needs. Design consultants and fashion co-ordinators may be employed on a regular or periodic basis. In an increasingly international market, a design

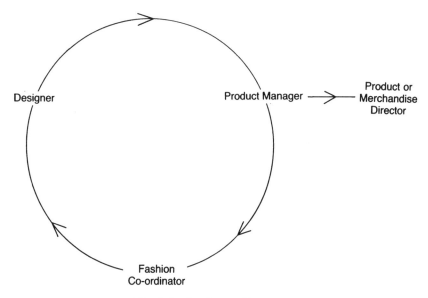

Fig. 3.3 Product cell concept.

consultant may be employed by a number of companies in different countries, all operating in the same product area but not generally in competition. At the high fashion end this continual injection of new ideas is seen as a way of avoiding staleness. High fashion designers who have achieved international reputations, particularly from countries such as France, Italy or the United Kingdom, simply sell their services to clothing organisations operating in lower priced markets.

The development of the matrix structure has resulted in, or perhaps has been the consequence of, the increasing importance of the whole marketing concept attached to clothing. The result has been to break up the traditional clothing company with its hierarchical structure, and to produce organisations in which the various functions from design through to production are separate. Thus a company may be essentially a marketing operation, with product managers employing outside designers and outside production units. Alternatively, an organisation may simply be a production unit contracting to a variety of product managers fed by designers. Increasingly, those production units are in low labour cost countries such as the Far East. Many famous brand name clothing organisations exist solely as marketing operations with their production sub-contracted to low labour cost countries. In addition to employing designers, within the organisation or on an outside consultancy basis, the company employs production specialists essentially to oversee and control the production in sub-contracted factories in other countries. Whatever the organisational structure in financial terms, however, the problem remains the same –

to create the necessary design and innovation within acceptable performance standards, and at a manufacturing cost which allows the product to be sold at a suitable price for the market.

Retail organisations

The situation is further complicated in the clothing industry, as indeed in other consumer product areas, by the enormous strength of many of the retail organisations, led in the UK by the chain stores. In the UK this has resulted in a position where a small number of retailers control over 50 per cent of the market. These retailers are not passive recipients of ideas from manufacturing organisations; they are actively involved in design and product development and marketing on their own behalf. In some cases retail organisations own manufacturing organisations. Indeed, in the UK the majority of clothing manufacturers are either closely allied to a large retail organisation or have a retail outlet of their own.

The interaction between the clothing manufacturer, which may have its own brand name to support, and a retail customer, which may or may not be part of the same company, can be extremely complex. The traditional retailer had two functions: first, the operation of the actual means of retail distribution, usually shops or mail order (directly or through an agent); and secondly the actual acquisition of the goods to be sold, or the buying operation. In a small retail operation the two were combined, but as the organisation grew the functions would be separated. In large retail organisations with hundreds of outlets the buying operation would be centralised and distinct from the store management which could only sell what the central buying operation acquired, and at the prices and in the manner dictated by them.

Within the buying organisation there would be a variety of buyers responsible for different product areas. They could be regarded as product managers, although certainly not in the same sense as in the manufacturing organisation. Nevertheless, the buyer's function is to search out markets and find suppliers capable of delivering the goods, which the retail organisation can then sell to the target market – again with the right combination of aesthetics, performance and price. Buyers may choose to work through the design and sales department of a manufacturer, but may also wish to contribute design ideas of their own or those acquired by the use of their own design department or design consultants. Where the retail buyer is the major customer of a particular manufacturing organisation, the manufacturer may come to rely on that buyer to provide design ideas. Such a relationship can be disastrous for the manufacturing organisation if the retail organisation withdraws its support, but equally the retail organisation may find the buyer is taking on some aspects of the work the manufacturer should carry out. It is in effect acting as the designer for its suppliers.

Large retailers have set up their own design departments but these stand in relation to the buyers rather as the traditional departments of a hierarchical structure stand in relation to the product managers in the matrix. If the manufacturing organisation insists on the buyers using its own design department, conflicts will arise between the buyers and the design department and complaints will be made about efficiency. If the buyers do not use the design department, it may be an expensive luxury.

The situation becomes more complex when a retail organisation owns its own production facility. Retailers essentially depend on variety and that incurs cost in production facilities. Again a retail organisation stands in relation to production rather as the product manager in manufacturing stands in relation to production in a matrix structure. Often the retail organisation will carry out its own design, i.e. the innovative stage, passing the design concept over to a product development operation which then transmits costings back to the retail organisation, together with made up samples for its approval. Where effective integration between retail and production has been achieved, usually by strong overall management, the results are extremely successful, particularly where high quality products are demanded and where a production unit has been attuned over a number of years to the requirements of its retail outlet.

However, conflict often occurs and the variety which the retail organisation needs may mean that the production facility concentrates on one aspect of this only, allowing the retail organisation to look for other production capability elsewhere. The production facility may then find itself short of orders and with excess production capacity; therefore it will start to look for customers outside its own retail organisation. In many cases this will be one of the large chain stores and the scene is set for a conflict of interests.

In the 1960s and 1970s the industry in the UK, as far as manufacturing was concerned, began to move towards large vertical groupings in which textile companies and clothing companies were integrated with the idea of all through production. In some situations retailers were involved. While many of these large groupings remain, the problems of managing the process have tended to force apart the links in the chain. Even where a clothing manufacturer is dependent for part of its textile supply on a company within the same group, it inevitably deals with suppliers outside the group. The same is true of clothing manufacturers and retailers.

As the innovative aspects of design become increasingly important, the difficulty of achieving that innovation and the constant stimulus which it needs tend to preclude permanent relationships between different sections of the trade and affect the organisation even within traditional trade boundaries. Yet, paradoxically, none can function without the others and while it may not be design or cost effective for them to operate as one company, the interaction between them must be successful if the consumer market is to be satisfied and the demand for clothing is to remain at its present level or develop.

For in essence the clothing industry has long since ceased to depend on the satisfaction of needs. It depends on the creation of wants, greatly in excess of actual need. If the organisational structure of the industry fails to generate the design and product innovation which will interest the consumer market, the future for all is bleak.

4

Quality Control

Quality control in clothing manufacture has in the past tended to mean final inspection with a little 'in process' inspection sometimes added. On the other hand, Total Quality Control hinges on creating an awareness of quality achievement throughout the whole business. It includes inspection routines of course, but relies much more on emphasising to everyone in the company that aspects of their job influence the finished quality of their product.

Quality assurance

The term 'quality assurance' is a phrase which is increasingly used in relation to the maintenance of quality. In general there are two different generic uses of the term. The first, generally termed 'quality control', is characterised by attention to issues arising from the production of garments, rather than to issues deriving from the original design or the design of the production process itself. Responsibility for quality rests with inspectors rather than with the designers or production staff. It is a system commonly employed in the clothing industry, where frequent changes of design occur, especially in women's fashion garments and where the original specifications are either sketchy or non-existent. The reject rate is high and this is backed up by an extensive repair system. This 'output' model of quality control is very wasteful, and when it is coupled to a system in which faults are returned frequently to machinists, or deductions made from payment, it can reduce motivation.

The second model of quality assurance can be characterised by the phrase, 'Quality cannot be inspected into a garment, it must be manufactured into it'. This can be applied on three levels. First and most simply, defects are traced back to the production process and the causes eliminated. This could involve the purchase of a special machine at one extreme or simply machine adjustment at the other. It could involve the lack of skill in the operator and the need for retraining. The second level, which is more comprehensive, is often termed 'Total

Quality Control'. Here the need for sustained quality performance is acknowledged to involve all relevant areas of the organisation and its suppliers. This is the basis of British Standard 5750, where the need to specify quality requirements extends not only through the company but also to its suppliers, in agreements about specifications and levels of monitoring their product. Thirdly, company-wide quality control requires the commitment of individuals in all departments, not just in production, focused by methods such as quality circles.

In other industries the development of these quality assurance models has been facilitated by increasingly sophisticated production, including robotics and reduced reliance on the human hand. Although the development of robotics has been very limited in clothing manufacture, that is no reason for abandoning attempts at more comprehensive quality assurance. The general aim is to decrease dependence on inspection as a means of achieving quality and to reduce the need to inspect all garments, by building quality into the garment in the first place. This is a change from a short-term, reactive method of quality assurance to a long-term project which is always capable of improvement to meet the present and future needs of the customer.

It is useful to consider quality control as a cycle in eight sections, as detailed below, which begins and ends with the customer.

Study of customer requirements

In the clothing industry customer requirements cannot by any means be described solely in functional quantitative terms such as the strength of a seam, the size of a pocket or the flexural rigidity of an interlining. They must in varying degrees meet the dictates of fashion. Clothing may also express status, the activity of the wearer or the donning of a uniform, and costume, representing something the wearer is not. The clothing industry tends to operate in fairly well defined price bands in which a number of companies compete. It is important for a company to define accurately the garment properties expected in its price band.

Satisfactory design of the garment

The design will achieve aesthetic objectives (see Chapter 2). The design process must also overcome the problem of fit. Bespoke garments are cut to fit an individual whose measurements and figure characteristics are known before manufacturing begins. Ready-to-wear garments are cut to fit categories of people whose measurements and figure characteristics are not known individually before manufacturing begins. The degree of fit which results is often therefore in some sense approximate, but it must be close enough, with or without alteration, to satisfy the customers' requirements. The concept of fit might imply different ideas from one garment to another: loose enough with a nightdress, tight enough with jeans, or the improvement of the figure by camouflaging or enhancing bust size. A satisfactory design of garment involves the cutting of not one, but a range of sizes. To satisfy the requirements of a range of sizes the design process must have an attitude toward a national system of size coding, and must decide what body measurements in its garments will be represented by the coding, what additions to make to body measurements for ease and comfort in wear, and what allowances to make for different styling features.

A satisfactory design of garment also demands decisions concerning the method of assembly. The designer will choose the seam type and stitch type which give the best combination of aesthetics, strength, elasticity, durability and so on. Choice of fusible often involves a design compromise between strength of bond on the one hand and an aesthetically pleasing result on the other, with the least 'rustle' and stiffness of handle.

It is particularly important for a satisfactory design that the garment be proved by adequate testing. The number of tests undertaken relates to the level of innovation in the garment and its components. The tests for fit and size cannot be other than trying the garments on as many different figures as possible to check that the designed effect is maintained. The tests of the fabric and trims are described in Chapter 5. The test for seam strength holds the opposing edges of a seam in clamps which are pulled apart, while the force required to cause rupturing is measured. Methods of testing the bond strength of fusibles are particularly important since a simple visual examination will tell little about the efficiency of the bond; tests measure the force required to strip the outer fabric from the fusible. The washing or dry-cleaning tests of whole garments provide a check of fusible, fabric and sewing. Wearer tests, looking at both comfort and durability, are commonly used with processes such as durable creasing and pleating.

Requirements of the design

Fabric specification

The first need is to specify the requirements of the components. If the sewing room sews on buttons by machine, the hole spacing is critical. If the garments are 'permanent press', the dyes must resist dye migration in the curing process. Below is an example of a fabric specification:

- Five pieces of polyester/wool worsted fabric.
- Length 70 m ± 10 m, to yield a total length of 350 m.
- Actual length to be not less than that stated on the invoice.
- Width 150 cm ± 1 cm.
- Weigh 200 g/m ± 15 g/m.
- Ends 25 per cm ± 1.
- Picks 25 per cm ± 1.
- Weave structure 2/2 twill.
- Fibre 65 per cent polyester/35 per cent wool.
- Shrinkage potential 1 per cent in warp and weft (according to WIRA Steam Cylinder Test).
- Shade and surface properties according to sample.

Garment specification

A design or garment specification commonly includes the following items:

(1) A description of the style features, with an illustration.
(2) A description of fabric limits and which fabrics may be made up into this garment style. Often the answer is one design of fabric in a range of colours; at the other extreme the answer is several hundred fabric designs. What is important is that, for instance, a fabric with low twist yarns is not asked to accept cut through pockets.
(3) The trims required. This includes the exterior trims which are features of the style as well as inside trims which influence the silhouette, such as shoulder pads.
(4) A size scale in which the style will be manufactured.
(5) Critical garment dimensions and tolerances. This is usually published as a size chart, relating key measurements to the codings in the size scale. The critical measurements relate to fit. Tolerance is the amount by which a garment may deviate from the correct measurements and still be acceptable. A dress is designed to measure say 150 cm from neck to finished hem. The designer has several choices of tolerance: ±1 cm, ±2 cm, +2 cm, +4 cm. The decision is a compromise between providing consistency and the cost of achieving a fine tolerance in manufacture.
(6) A specification of stitch and seam types to be used.
(7) Relevant details of the process. This may include both a description of method and notes on machinery and attachments. The difficulty here is how much to include, because the regular or standard details of the process are recorded in another form. The question asked by the designer who writes the specification should

be: what instruction is necessary before the factory can achieve an accurate copy of the design?

Manufacturing specification

The third sort of specification is a manufacturing specification, which relates to operations and processes rather than individual garment styles. A list of categories might include the name by which the operation is to be known, the materials to be used (described by shape, fabric type, dimensions, shade and so on), the thread, relevant details of the machine (stitch type, needle size, maximum stitching speed, work aids and attachments), the method to be carried out – recorded element by element – and key points of quality.

On blindstitching hems, for instance, this would include stitch density, position of stitching in relation to edge of turnup, whether on 'skip' or not, where sewing begins and amount of overrun at finish, seams in turnup lying on seams of outer fabric, no rucking or fullness in hem, width of hem as specified and the same all the way round, no stitches or impressions showing in the outer fabric (some fabrics are so hard that minimum impressions have to be tolerated), and final thread end through the correct loop to secure the stitching.

The designer plays an important role in developing all three types of specification. The content of a specification is often the result of negotiation with other functions in a business, but it is the designer who puts it all together as a record of decisions taken.

Meeting design requirements

It must be confirmed that the manufacturing processes and materials are capable of meeting the design requirements. This is required because samples are frequently made in a sample room or in other special conditions and the objective is to complete a satisfactory sample for a range meeting. Bulk output may not be manufactured by the same methods or machinery, and certainly not by a sophisticated and knowledgeable sample machinist. Hence the confirmation checks both machinery and the skills of operators. Production management checks that:

- Fabric has the required stability, resistance to fray, resistance to glazing by presses and so on;
- Blindstitch machines are capable of sewing a new fabric without the stitch appearing on the outside of the garment;
- The designer has not created a feature so difficult to sew that operators cannot hope to achieve consistency (and there is no way

of simplifying the method). Often a trial batch brings problems to light before the factory launches into full production (if there is time).

Meeting standards

There must be a full acceptance, by all those concerned with production, of their responsibility for meeting the standards set by the specification. In the restricted meaning of 'quality control', responsibility for quality rests with inspectors rather than with designers or production staff. This can lead to a high rate of rejects, and minor faults are overlooked. This 'output' approach is backed up by an extensive repair system and is wasteful; in addition, if too many defects are returned to machinists they lose motivation.

On the other hand, total quality control acknowledges that sustained quality performance involves all relevant areas of the organisation and its suppliers. This is the basis of British Standard 5750, where the need to specify quality requirements extends not only through the company but also by agreement to all the suppliers in the chain. Total quality control involves an acceptance by all managers and all operators of an agreed division of responsibility for the quality of the finished garment. The responsibilities of the operator are: to refuse acceptance of incorrect work into the operation, to carry out the agreed method for the job, to ensure that the garments completed are of the agreed standard, and to resew defective garments returned for repair. The responsibilities of the supervisor could be written in almost the same way, but on a larger scale in relation to the section.

In theory difficulties are fed back to the designer so that garments may be improved, either by altering the design specification or controlling operators more strictly. Through the organisation of the 'quality circle', the drive for quality (and not only quality) is focused on the significant issues. The origin of the process is brainstorming sessions, followed by reporting sessions and a commitment by management to solve the problems identified. Quality is achieved through specifications, the responsibility of operators and the commitment of designer and management to make production operations as easy as possible. This means that assembly workers meet with management at regular intervals to discuss quality aspects and ideas for the improvement of the product. In Britain this idea has met with limited success. It tries to lift an organisation from Japanese culture to a different Western culture. Employees are unwilling to operate quality circles outside normal hours and the piecework method of payment tends to produce a culture where changes in specification are viewed primarily in terms of whether there will be a benefit through the payment system, rather than in terms of whether the company will benefit in terms of improved quality.

Check on garments

There are three objectives of inspecting garments to see that they conform with the specification: to protect the customer from recurring defective garments, to safeguard the reputation of the company in the market and to provide information about failure to conform to specifications. The last of these is the most important in the continuing drive to improve quality performance. Feedback from inspection at any stage of manufacture provides a criticism of design, manufacturing methods and the organisation of inspection itself.

Part of this inspection is directed at incoming goods. Deliveries are checked against specifications. In some situations it is possible to negotiate with suppliers a contract in which they are responsible for the inspection, perhaps on a sampling basis, and then forwarding the records of the inspection with the delivery. If the clothing manufacturer checks the incoming goods, he will concentrate on those factors which feedback has shown to be a problem. This might include dimensional stability, colour fastness or fibre composition. Textile goods are not consistent; these three properties can vary from delivery to delivery. Performance properties should be checked not only with the customer in mind but also to improve performance in manufacturing. A change in dimensions leads to under or over sizing and loss of output. Small samples of fabric can be checked relatively easily for dimensional stability, using a washing machine, steam press or, more formally, a WIRA Steam Cylinder. Colour fastness can be monitored simultaneously. Finishes such as resin treatment of cotton and viscose can also vary from batch to batch. This treatment affects both washing performance and durability. A simple tear strength test on a sample from each delivery establishes whether the finish and fabric are correct.

If the trouble which might occur in manufacture without checks will cost more than the inspection, then the inspection is worthwhile. One of the principal problems is localised fabric faults, such as slubs, holes and stains. Formerly these faults were identified by strings attached to the selvedge. This method was useful but not entirely satisfactory. The textile manufacturer's concept of fault did not always coincide with that of the garment manufacturer or his customer. Contractual arrangements meant that if a fabric had more than a given number of strings, the supplier would give compensation by an allowance of a length of fabric per string. Often slubs were not strung, but a slub in a shirt collar would make the garment unsaleable. A hundred small slubs, not strung, would be a bigger problem than 10 strung holes.

Newer methods allocate points to faults, such as one for a small slub and five for a hole. These would be more effective if operated continuously. Shading and check bow and skew are also costly. Shading may occur from piece to piece, from end to end of a piece or from side to side of a piece. Inspection for shading depends on inspectors with a high level of discrimination in all hues, the right lighting and background (sometimes the same as the retail store) and well defined standards of what is acceptable. A special difficulty occurs with side to side shading. Often this can only be seen after two parts have been sewn into a seam and it is pressed open. Hence one test cuts a six inch strip across the piece, divides it into four, mixes up the four and sews and presses open three seams, in order to give a clear view of any shading.

One defence for the manufacturer is to carry out vendor rating, through sampling the supply from all suppliers. This builds up a picture of the quality performance of all the suppliers so that an alternative may be sought where necessary.

Where garments are not being manufactured to the correct size, there can be a number of causes. The manufacturer will check whether the garments bear the correct ticket, the width of seams, whether overlockers have shaved off more than a few fibres (look under the machine), the tightness of plies in spreading in the cutting room (distortions in spreading are likely to be worse with knitted or stretch fabrics), any 'shaving' in the marker, the dimensional stability of the fabric itself and finally the dimensions of the pattern. Distortions in spreading are particularly troublesome because the fabric may recover only later during making up or even in dry-cleaning. With all these factors involved, where operations are operator-controlled, it is very difficult to achieve perfectly accurate dimensions. Hence a defined amount of tolerance is usually given. One method is to give both a positive and negative tolerance, for example ±1 cm on a garment length. Unless there is very tight control, this could lead to the toleration of under sizing. A safer view is that tolerances should all be positive, which means that the pattern and the manufacturing process aim to produce a finished garment which is half the tolerance too big. How much the tolerance should be is a matter for the designer's judgement in each case.

Inspection during making up is carried out in process, at the final stage or by roving inspectors, or a combination of all three. The method chosen is governed by cost effectiveness. Wherever the cost of rectifying faults at final inspection is greater than the cost at an intermediate stage, the case for in process inspection can be sustained. Inspection does not of course end with the sewing operations, but may also take place at pressing and before despatch. This last inspection is often carried out by a specialist recruited from a retail background, whose task is threefold: to check against the order that the customer will receive precisely what was ordered, that all the garments are the same (not a silly task when one set of buttons may be a reasonable match but different from the rest), and that all the labels required are present and correct (labels are a big sub-industry within garment manufacture).

The designer seeks to ensure a rational and effective organisation of inspection resources, may press for increased resources and will often influence the training and attitudes of inspectors. It is the inspectors who in the end ensure the reputation of the designer's products and of the company; but more importantly the inspectors provide information about failure to conform to the specifications. It is essential for the designer to monitor the performance of all garment styles in order that appropriate modifications may be made.

Instructions

Instruction in the use, application and limitations of the garment takes the form of sewing on labels which instruct the customer in the care of the garment. The first type, fibre content, are a legal requirement and in the UK must quote generic names (there are thousands of brand names of fibres worldwide). The reason for this is partly that, while two generations ago our grandparents recognised wool, linen and cotton and knew how to care for them, many new fibres need different treatments.

The second type is not a legal requirement, but very few garments do not carry a care label with some sort of instructions. The range of instructions may cover temperature of wash, degree of agitation, drying (do not tumble dry acrylics for the garments shrink), bleaching, ironing, and dry-cleaning in usually one of two fluids. This label is the entry card to a cleaning system which includes the garment, the washing cycle, the drying cycle and ironing temperatures or alternatively dry-cleaning. In theory the system is rational and effective, but in practice there are a few drawbacks.

Some manufacturers may be over cautious in their specification of washing temperature. It is a question of how frequently a person sorts the washing at home into all the possible piles and carefully goes through each cycle. In practice, according to admittedly anecdotal evidence, people use at most two and occasionally another one. Evidence gathered in a private survey outside large retail chainstores suggests a surprising ignorance among the general public about the meaning of the labels, and an instinctive approach to selecting a washing cycle or simply using the same one all the time.

User experience and feedback

Many companies respect customers' complaints and generally reimburse the customer without question. The certainty of reimbursement should concentrate the efforts of the manufacturing department on finding the cause of the defect which led to the complaint. One customer's complaint may represent many other customers who do not complain and the company must take notice until it can prove this is an isolated case. Thus the cycle of quality control returns to its starting point – a study of customers' requirements. Ultimately quality assessment is in the hands of the customer and therefore complaints from customers are of paramount importance in determining whether an adequate quality assurance scheme operates. Too often quality controllers see a complaints department as a judgement on their own efficiency, rather than as part of the whole quality control operation.

There are many causes of customer complaint but one common cause is the breaking of a factory habit or routine. A rare complaint is a garment without buttons; this is almost invariably a garment which has been rectified on the line, has then become late or overdue for delivery, has been re-pressed in a hurry and disappeared before the buttons could be replaced. A more frequent complaint is burst seams. Setting aside the size of the wearer, a common explanation is a join in the seam clearly following a break in the thread while sewing. The operator has over run the first sewing for, say, 2–3 inches but instead of sewing parallel has sewn at a narrow angle to the first sewing, thus creating a weak spot where the two lines cross.

While some customers' complaints may be unjustified in terms of what can reasonably be expected of a garment (and may occasionally be fraudulent), an efficient quality assurance operation separating the justified from the unjustified and feeding the information back to design, manufacturing and inspection systems can only benefit the company's quality and its image. What is attainable is a comprehensive quality assurance scheme which is not continually diverted by short term expediency. The common problem of whether to use a delivery of fabric known to be faulty, because if it is not used delivery of garments will be late to the customer, can only be avoided if the specifications on which the contract to buy is based are thoroughly planned and established. To achieve this sort of paradigm requires total management commitment to quality.

It is the responsibility of the designer to decide the content and indeed the format of all the labels included in a garment.

The designer and quality control

This chapter gives a somewhat formal outline of quality control, because the achievement of quality targets is crucial to success in marketing, and therefore the attitudes and methods of quality management penetrate all areas of a company's business. The designer plays a key role in the achievement of quality targets.

Two definitions need to be borne in mind at the beginning.

(1) Quality of design means the value inherent in the garment; the functional and perceived value of the materials (silk versus cotton, polyester/wool versus polyester/viscose, real mother-of-pearl and horn buttons and so on), and the amount of work content (a lined versus an unlined skirt, the number of pockets in a suit, taped hems versus overlocked hems).
(2) Quality of conformity means the faithfulness with which the output conforms to the design concept, or more simply the incidence of defects.

Quality of design is a combination of aesthetics, performance and price, appropriate to the individual customer; obtaining a good balance

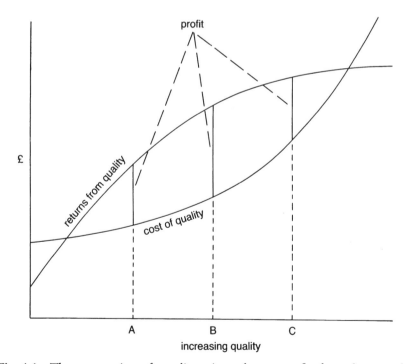

Fig. 4.1 The economics of quality: A = lower profit from lower sales revenue; B = maximum profit; C = lower profit from higher costs.

of these is the chief requirement of good design. Quality of conformity means that it is essential that this quality is maintained in the individual garments produced against the original design. The problem is maintaining consistency in bulk production in a factory amidst the pressures of achieving production targets, operator variability and a variety of machinery needing continual repair and maintenance. Except at the top end of the market, customers do not buy the original design but a mass produced copy. Their concept of the original design, their satisfaction with the product, and hence their tendency to return for a repurchase to the producer or the retailer, depends on that copy.

Faults – properties the customer cannot accept – can be traced to the original design or to the copying. In either case any scheme for the maintenance of quality must ensure not only the rectification of faults occurring during production but also a feedback system to ensure that they do not occur again.

The responsibilities of the designer of course include all aspects of quality of design. The designer must compare the cost of achieving the value in the garment with the returns from this quality – the price that can be charged. As value increases, the price a company can charge increases, but ever more slowly. Costs are the opposite and the costs of fabric, trims and work content increase ever more quickly (Fig. 4.1). In any company's range of options there is a point of maximum profit. Below this point a lesser profit comes from the lower price a company can charge; above this point a lower profit comes from the higher costs involved.

The designer also has responsibilities in the area of quality of conformity. In simple terms the garments must be as easy as possible to make within the requirements of the given style. Standardisation is a dirty word in a fashion industry, but there are some ways to categorise the variety. For instance, there are relationships which can be standardised. The relationship between the edge of a fusible interlining and the edge of the outer fabric should wherever possible be the same. Operators are more likely to form a habit and get it right. Similarly, notches on seams should be found in the same part of the seam. Wherever possible the two plies of a seam should have equal profiles, which is much easier to sew than joining a straight edge to a round edge or joining opposite curves. Of course, opposite curves as on a 'princess' line dress are sometimes unavoidable.

5

Materials

Balance of factors

For the majority of clothing items aesthetic factors provide the initial impulse of attraction and may be the only factors which influence the decision to buy. The exception is the requirement that the item should fit. But even fit may be a function of fashion and style. Such aesthetic factors as handle, drape, colour and style all interact in a complex manner and are crudely and subtly influenced by social factors – a desire to be seen to be in fashion, a desire to present an image, for example.

Clearly there are exceptions where performance is an over-riding consideration, as in protective clothing, even if only for a leisure pursuit. However, the comment by a customer that they do not consider performance when purchasing is quite frequently correct. That does not, of course, mean that performance is unimportant to them. Premature breakdown, whether of fabric, seam or simply a button falling off, may produce a customer complaint, and although the customer may not actually return the garment to the retailer, it may well result in an association in their mind of poor performance, which may influence their decision on another purchase.

Aesthetic and performance factors are, of course, inextricably linked with price. The often-repeated statement that 'you get what you pay for' is generally associated with performance, but a customer's concept of what the level of performance should be will vary considerably. It is often influenced by aesthetic considerations. Thus the concept of good quality is not a static issue operating at one level for all customers; it is influenced by aesthetics, performance and price, and is specific to an individual customer. An example of this is a silk tie. To most customers this would represent good quality, but in performance terms silk is markedly inferior to polyester. A polyester tie, however, would be considered of lower quality than a silk tie and, of course, would be cheaper. In this situation aesthetic characteristics are dominating the opinion expressed. This leads to a number of guidelines about the balance between aesthetics, performance and price:

(1) For a given customer the balance required will change with the item being purchased. A woman, for example, may apply very different criteria to the purchase of a dress for a social occasion from those applied to the purchase of a pair of school trousers for her son.

(2) Balance is dependent on the socio-economic position of the customer. Higher income group people will be willing to pay a high price for individuality in aesthetic terms and will be less concerned about durability, although they may expect high performance standards for the albeit short lifespan of the item. Quality is not a single definable entity; it is a statement of the balance of factors which will satisfy an individual customer.

(3) Overall economic factors may radically change the behaviour of customers in terms of perceived requirements. Credit restrictions and a harsh economic climate may not only lead to reduced purchase but also to greater attention to performance details such as durability.

An item of clothing is a summation of materials, starting with fibre, through yarn, fabric and trimmings which go to make it up. The complexities of balancing aesthetics, performance and cost factors therefore apply to the selection and use of these materials. Customers have perceptions of the aesthetic and performance values of all components of clothing items, although of course their judgement may be faulty and subject to misunderstood technical factors as well as ingrained social habits. The classic example is the belief that wool is 'warm'. The fact that wool garments constructed and designed in an appropriate way do give a high level of insulation does not mean that other fibres used in different constructions and with a wider variety of applications may not give insulation in a far more cost-effective way. Nevertheless, the tradition of a wool overcoat remains and represents a level of social standing.

We will now look at the materials used in the construction of clothing, in terms of their availability and their actual and perceived properties. This is not designed to be a detailed exposition of textile fibre and textile technology.

Fibres

All textile fibres are complex long-chain polymers. The difference between them is in the chemical nature of the polymer and in the physical structure. A number are made of the same polymer, cellulose, but while they are similar in many ways, there are also considerable differences caused by the way in which the chemical cellulose is physically arranged to produce the fibre. Examples are cotton, linen, viscose and modal.

The terms 'natural', 'regenerated' and 'synthetic' fibres – the last two being grouped together as man-made – refer to the origin of the polymer. Natural fibres are obtained directly from a plant or animal and, apart from cleaning processes, are used largely as they occur naturally. Regenerated fibres are those made from a natural polymer, almost invariably cellulose, which has either been regenerated in a fibre form (as in viscose from woodpulp) or has been subjected to some chemical modification and then spun in fibre form (as in acetate and triacetate). Synthetic fibres are made by industrial processes from polymers which have been built up from simple chemicals; these chemicals, almost invariably, come from oil.

Natural fibres

In general, natural fibres score on aesthetics, are variable in performance and are tending to become higher in price. Some are very expensive. Regenerated fibres have a poor aesthetic image and poor performance but are cheap. Synthetic fibres have good performance and are relatively cheap, despite the vagaries of the oil market, but are not good aesthetically.

The most important natural fibre is *cotton* which accounts for about 50 per cent of world fibre usage, although in western Europe and the USA it has been overtaken by polyester. Although growing is limited to frost-free areas, cotton is widely produced all over the world and owes part of its popularity to the fact that the seed from which the cotton fibres are detached in processing is a valuable source of oil and protein, both of which can be used as a foodstuff. Cotton has a good aesthetic image and is believed to be comfortable to wear (related to its ability to absorb moisture); but it has several performance drawbacks, notably the need for ironing unless it is resin treated, and its high flammability. Although the cheapest of the natural fibres, the price movement is upwards as land values and labour costs rise even in under-developed countries. It is now more expensive than polyester.

Linen is another natural fibre based on cellulose, although very different aesthetically from cotton. It is much more expensive to produce than cotton and does not perform as well, but the linen appearance – which can be copied by using regenerated fibres – and the handle produced by certain finishing processes, still give it an aesthetic appeal.

There are a large number of other natural fibres derived from cellulose, such as hemp, manilla and jute, but none of these has significant use in clothing. Although they are cheap, the handle is generally too harsh and unattractive for clothing; they are more suited to their use in ropes, carpets etc.

After cotton, the next significant natural fibre is *wool*. It has a high aesthetic image, although only in Western Europe, Japan and parts of the USA. Customers overestimate the performance qualities of wool, although for certain types of outer wear it is the most acceptable fibre. It is becoming increasingly expensive, however, partly through economic manipulations of the market since production is virtually static.

There are several other natural fibres derived from animal hair, the most important being mohair, alpaca, cashmere and llama. All have high aesthetic appeal, particularly in the upper end of the market, and are used either as substitutes for, or in blends with, wool. World production is limited, although there is no problem concerning animal rights since the animals do not need to be killed in order to obtain the fibre. This is not the case with the vicuna goat for here, although the yield is a highly prized fibre, the animal does generally die. While the price is high, fibre sometimes becomes available more cheaply when, for example, an under-developed country wishes to obtain foreign currency and releases relatively large quantities on to the market. This occasionally happens with cashmere.

Another fibre which is generally expensive but sometimes dumped on the world market is *silk*. Despite this its high aesthetic value remains undiminished. It does, however, have considerable drawbacks in terms of creasing particularly when wet. For this reason, even when the price is relatively low and the market expands, there is soon customer reaction against the use of silk in, for example, blouses and shirts.

Regenerated fibres

The first man-made fibres were regenerated but their popularity has gradually receded. The main regenerated fibre is viscose (the former name rayon is not permissible). Its performance is markedly inferior to cotton, particularly in wet strength, although it is cheaper. Its former market, such as linings, has gradually been lost but it is still popular for certain print fabrics for blouses and dresses, as well as in household textiles. It is always cheaper than cotton, although where demand for cotton greatly exceeded supply it might manage price comparability.

A better fibre than viscose in performance terms but closely related to it is modal. This is stronger than viscose and much nearer cotton in performance although, of course, it cannot be used under that name. Its price is generally between that of cotton and viscose.

Two other regenerated fibres are made by chemically modifying cellulose: acetate and triacetate. Both are cheap and both have been promoted with a fashion image. Acetate was used extensively for cheap linings but is now largely superseded. Performance is markedly inferior to polyester and nylon and the price difference is not now very great. The main attraction is aesthetic. Acetate was formerly known as artificial silk but that term is now illegal. It has some of the characteristics of that natural fibre and is capable of giving bright coloured prints.

Synthetic fibres

By far the most important man-made fibre, and second only to cotton in total world usage, is polyester. It has a high standard of performance, except in terms of moisture absorption, but its aesthetic image has suffered with the change in the social climate towards natural fibres. It is, however, cheaper than all the natural fibres, and although it is subject to oil price changes and, therefore, like all fibres subject to opportunistic pricing by the market, it is likely to retain its popularity.

For clothing, nylon (generally now known as polyamide) has yielded the lead to polyester. The reasons for this are partly aesthetic – i.e. the association of nylon with the warp knitted fabrics of 20 years ago – but also include important technological differences in processing and in ability to blend with other fibres. Two varieties of nylon are generally used, known as 66 and 6, but from a consumer performance viewpoint these are indistinguishable. Commercial production now is geared more towards 6 because production is cheaper. The performance of nylon is at least comparable with that of polyester.

Acrylic fibre retains a significant market share as an alternative to wool, particularly in knitwear. It can be extremely price competitive with wool and it does have the advantage over the natural fibre that it is machine washable. This advantage has been partly eliminated by the machine washable finishes now available for wool, but the price difference remains. Essentially, the decision is based on price versus aesthetics.

Some use has been made commercially of polyethylene and polypropylene fibres, particularly the latter, but they both suffer the grave disadvantage that they melt at temperatures not much greater than 100°C. This is below the normal cool setting on a domestic iron. The low price and relatively good properties, although suffering from the usual poor aesthetics of synthetics, have not been sufficient to overcome the problem of melting.

The other synthetic fibre of note is a very specialised one: elastane. This is now almost universally used as a substitute for rubber, and because it does not have the same deterioration characteristics has enabled a wide variety of stretch garments to be produced. Although expensive, it is used in small quantities within the material and therefore can give marketing advantages of stretch for a relatively low price increase.

Filament and staple

Fibres may be available in two forms – filament or staple. The natural fibres, with the exception of silk, are all in staple form, whereas man-made fibres can, in theory, be produced in both. In practice, market considerations now mean that viscose is available generally only in staple form, with acetate and triacetate in filament. Acrylic is invariably staple but polyester and nylon are available in both.

Blends

The balance of aesthetics, performance and price in the choice of fibres has inevitably led to the production of blends. The objective is to achieve an optimum level at which the factors are balanced but the decision is often weighted by the relative importance of one factor.

Many of the present blends include polyester which gives a performance level with relatively low cost. It is allied to wool and cotton for aesthetic reasons. Some blends are designed to impart a specific property like the addition of elastane for stretch. The difficulty is determining the exact percentage of each fibre to incorporate in the blend. If the percentage is too low – generally less than 10 per cent except in the case of elastane – the property of the fibre would hardly be significant; although even here the psychological effect may be desirable, such as incorporating a low percentage of cashmere in a blend of wool.

It is important in evaluating a blend to decide the objective of that blend, for example the use of polyester with cotton. In the early days of this development the blends most favoured were 65 per cent or 67 per cent polyester, depending on the fibre producer, but the main aim of both was to achieve a dominant position for polyester in the blend, so maximising the use of the product and achieving optimum performance levels. The move towards natural fibres generated increased use of a 50 per cent polyester blend. This did not alter the performance significantly although it did increase the price, but it was certainly more acceptable to cotton producers.

The continuation of this trend has led to the so-called 'cotton rich blends' where the percentage of cotton at 55 per cent or 60 per cent is greater than that of polyester, thus allowing the name of cotton to feature first on the label under the Fibre Labelling Regulations. These Regulations do affect what can be done since they require the dominant fibre in a blend to be listed first, thus giving it the maximum marketing impact.

Blends may, therefore, have a variety of origins: lower price, as in the incorporation of viscose and to some extent polyester; enhanced performance, as in the incorporation of polyester and nylon; and improved aesthetics, as in the incorporation of wool or silk. Blends with a wide variety of fibres may simply result from the price advantage of re-using fibres reclaimed from scrap garments, as in the cheap woollen type fabrics often used in skirtings.

Yarns

Staple fibres generally require conversion into yarns as the first stage in the production of fabric. The traditional names 'woollen' and 'worsted' refer to spinning systems used to deal with wool and are not, although they are often used as such, substitutes for the name wool. The woollen system gives high bulk yarns with relatively lower strength and the worsted system high twist yarns with relatively higher strength. In fact, synthetic fibres may be processed on both these systems, as indeed they may be on the system originally designed for cotton.

The growth in the use of man-made fibres has caused many modifications in the traditional spinning systems to enable them to operate more efficiently with synthetic fibres. The general characteristics of the cotton system and the woollen and worsted systems remain, but they are overlaid by the fibres or blends used on them. The requirements of a yarn with sufficient strength and aesthetic characteristics, such as bulk, are constantly weighed against the need to simplify the spinning process in order to reduce costs. Silk, although a filament fibre, can be spun using the Schappe system to give the equivalent of a staple yarn, but the process is relatively little used for fabric production.

Filament yarn can be used with little modification to produce fabric, but while its characteristic of flat, shiny, low bulk is a aesthetically acceptable for silk and lining materials generally, it is not considered aesthetically correct or desirable for many other types of apparel. Filament yarn users were therefore concerned to develop yarn which had bulk characteristics similar to those of staple fibre yarns. This was achieved through a variety of textured yarn processing systems, by far the most popular of which is the false twist method developed originally for nylon but used extensively on polyester. Recently another system, using air jets, has become popular for modifying filament nylon.

Although these textured processes do markedly change the aesthetic characteristics of flat filament yarn, the result is distinguishable from the conventional spun staple fibre. For example, 100 per cent polyester false twist textured is vastly different from 100 per cent polyester filament and very different again from 100 per cent polyester spun on the cotton system. The advantage, however, is that textured yarns are considerably cheaper than staple spun yarns as the process is far quicker. This has led to the continued popularity of 100 per cent textured polyester.

In addition to the standard type of yarn a large range of novelty or fancy effect yarns is possible, such as bouclé. These novelty yarns may combine two, three or more different yarns and are aimed solely at aesthetic effect. The problem is that the more work done in the production of a yarn, be it simply increasing twist or introducing variety, the higher the price. Twofold or even threefold yarns improve aesthetics and sometimes performance, but cost considerably more than a single yarn because of the extra twisting and processing involved. This also applies to novelty yarns and considerably reduces their usage except in occasional fashion outbursts.

Fabrics

The principal methods of converting yarn to fabric remain weaving and the two basic forms of knitting – warp and weft. Warp knitting became very important in the 1960s because it represented the fastest means then of converting yarn to fabric. Unfortunately the machinery was limited in that it could only use flat filament yarn, and although attempts have been made to modify warp knitting machines to incorporate staple fibre yarns these have generally not been commercially successful. The result, for aesthetic reasons, has been a decline in the popularity of warp knitting.

Weft knitting, however, has remained popular both for garment sections made to require minimum make-up, and as fabric used on a cut and sew basis. The large market generated in the 1960s and early 1970s for weft-knitted fabric based on textured polyester has greatly declined, but other forms of knitted goods continue in popularity. In performance terms the main difference is in the stretch capability. A weft-knitted fabric has, in general, considerably more stretch than a woven one, with warp-knitting coming in between. Different structures can cause variations on this but the general principle remains. Weft-knitting remains a faster process than weaving but looms have, with the replacement of the old shuttle, increased in productivity in the last 20 years so weaving is now reasonably competitive with knitting.

There remains the aesthetic evaluation by the customer of woven as opposed to knitted fabric and, except in knitwear, this has tended to favour wovens once the large price disadvantage was removed.

In performance terms, the density of yarn usage and the type of weave or knit structure considerably influence performance, not only in terms of stretch.

The main competitor to weaving and knitting in fabric production has been the rise of the so-called 'non-wovens'. The name generally applies to those fabrics where the conversion is direct from fibre to fabric, without the usual stages of yarn production. In practice the first stage of yarn production is followed with the manufacture of a web of fibres, and these are bonded together (hence the name bonded fibre fabrics) by a variety of mechanical and chemical means. The result is an extremely cheap form of fabric production but with significant aesthetic, in terms of customer perception, and performance drawbacks.

The aesthetics vary depending on the bonding method used but generally non-wovens are stiffer and less flexible and drape less well than the traditional woven or knitted structure. They have virtually no stretch and, generally, poor durability. Where price is a prime consideration, as in disposable garments, non-wovens have a ready market, but the move back towards the traditional textile image has lessened their impact on clothing which in the late 1960s and early 1970s appeared to be becoming significant.

While there are clear differences in general terms between woven, knitted and non-wovens, these difference can be offset as far as costs are concerned by the variety of structures and the density of yarns used. A closely woven or knitted structure made from fine yarns may be considerably more expensive than a heavier loosely woven or knitted structure made from bulky yarns, despite the fact that the latter will have considerably more fibre. The added value of the processing in yarn and fabric production will more than have off-set the cost of the fibre involved.

Dyeing and finishing

The use of dye stuffs to impart colour to textile fabrics can, in practice, be at any stage of the process. Dye may be added to the polymer mix before it is extruded as fibres, and this is one of the cheapest ways of incorporating colour. Unfortunately, it can only be done on a large scale and so the colours available in this way are limited to certain basics such as black. However, from time to time 'melt-spun' dyeing is used and may offer an advantageous method of obtaining basic colours.

The more usual point of dyeing is either fibres, to get mixture effect, yarn, to get stripes or checks, or of course piece dyeing of the whole fabric. Even here, pattern effects may be obtained by incorporating different fibres which will react differently to the dye. Here it is important to ensure that the fibres have similar characteristics in other performance respects, or different colour effects may result during wear. The combination of a strong and weak fibre may produce unwelcome dye changes. The usual fibres for this process are polyester and nylon.

Yarn dyeing is the most expensive method but it does give the best aesthetic result for stripes and checks. Processes occasionally become available for colouring yarns in a variety of coloured effects, often known as space dyeing. These methods, although giving an interesting aesthetic and sometimes fashionable appearance, are expensive.

The other method of imparting colour is, of course, printing. Although processes exist for printing both sides of a fabric (duplex), the general method is to print one side only. This obviously imposes some limitations in making up. As usual a balance has to be struck between aesthetic considerations in terms of sharpness of print and detail, and performance in terms of fastness and cost.

The cheapest method is probably roller printing but the definition here is not of the highest quality, although for long runs it is certainly the cheapest. The most generally used method of printing at present is rotary screen printing which gives high definition and, although usually more expensive than roller printing, becomes cheaper for short runs where the initial high cost of the roller would not be offset. This method has almost totally superseded the automatic flat screen method.

Transfer printing is capable of very high definition and relatively low cost, partly because the design may be held in paper form and only printed on to fabric in response to demand, thus obviating the possibility of unsold stock. However, it is limited to polyester or high percentage polyester blend fabrics.

Finishing processes are generally carried out on the fabric and can be conveniently sub-divided into those which affect aesthetics (generally physical processes), and those which affect performance (involving the addition of chemicals).

Physical processes such as brushing, cropping or calendering either raise or flatten the surface, not only affecting handle but also light reflectiveness. Most do not affect performance properties although increasing the thickness will increase the insulation. Chemical finishes, on the other hand, considerably alter performance. These may include finishes for fire resistance, waterproofing, ironing performance, improved washing performance and the release of soil. Any processing, physical or chemical, obviously increases the cost but the improvements in aesthetics and/or performance are usually regarded as worth the extra. The danger is that the process may have side-effects which damage other aesthetic or performance characteristics.

For example, the resin finish on cotton which greatly improves its ironing performance markedly reduces durability and gives a stiff and less attractive handle. On the other hand, at least 50 per cent of the added value of a fine wool worsted suiting fabric will come from the effort spent on improving its handle by physical finishing methods. Each finish must, therefore, be judged on its merits in altering the balance of aesthetic performance and price in relation to the market.

Trimmings

In the manufacture of clothing the main fabric is supplemented by a variety of trimmings whose number and complexity will depend on the type of garment. All garments will employ sewing thread in some form but additional items may be lining, interlining, tapes, labels, buttons and various other fastening devices including zips, and shoulder pads etc. The trimming may be for aesthetic reasons, performance reasons or a combination of both and it will have a cost which must be weighed against its advantages.

Most trimmings involve both functions. Buttons, for example, have a practical value but also increasingly have an aesthetic one. Zips as a means of fastening may be concealed because they are not considered aesthetically pleasing; alternatively, they may become a fashion feature. Any trimming should not detract from the performance characteristics of the main fabric.

Most trimmings are themselves textile materials, as in linings, interlinings and sewing thread. The most popular material for linings is now woven nylon or polyester, although woven viscose filament and occasionally acetate are still in use. Pockets generally include polyester or nylon for performance reasons. Interlinings are now largely fusible, often based on non-woven materials. Since these are almost inevitably concealed in the garment, their appearance is not important; they need to produce the right drape and handle, combined with a resistance to deformation. Fusible non-wovens give this at the lowest possible price both in initial cost and in manufacturing process. Traditionally, however, other types of interlining are still employed, especially in the tailoring industries.

Most sewing threads are now polyester, but they may contain small percentages of cotton. Cotton sewing thread, although used, is increasingly losing ground because of the price as well as performance advantage of polyester. Apart from a small amount of nylon and a limited amount of silk for decorative purposes, no other fibre is significant in sewing thread.

Make-up

Manufacturing a garment from a fabric is the conversion of a flat two-dimensional form into a three-dimensional shape to fit the human body. In the majority of cases this is done by cutting pieces to defined shapes and joining them in such a way that the three-dimensional form is built up. The way in which this is done and the position of the seams are often dictated by aesthetics or, particularly in menswear, by traditional views of where these seams should be. In tailoring, some underwear manufacturing and millinery, a limited amount of shape is produced by moulding or shaping. Obviously the more seams and the more complex they are, the greater the cost, but this may be accepted for aesthetic reasons. For example, in shirt manufacture a lap-fell seam is considered more acceptable than the much cheaper overlock safety stitch seam.

A variety of stitches are available for joining garment sections, primarily concerned with producing sufficient strength and, in the case of woven fabrics, preventing fraying of edges; but, as previously mentioned, the final selection may be dictated by aesthetics. Lock-stitch (301) is the most common joining seam but chain stitch (2-thread) may be used in bulk production where long seam runs give it a competitive advantage (see Chapter 4).

The final process in making up – pressing – is carried out to obtain the desired aesthetic appearance in the new garment. Indeed, pressing may take place at various stages during the garment construction in order to achieve the desired effect. Pressing may also be needed to impart pleats or creases which are required as part of the convention for that garment, for example in trousers. Again, the duration of pressing and in particular the amount of under pressing greatly adds to the cost of the garment but may be considered essential in order that the garment presents the right image at the point of sale.

Sourcing

Between any two stages in the processes leading from fibre to finished garment or indeed retail, a buying and selling opportunity exists. Although organisations have been set up which attempt a vertical integration from fibre through to finished garment or beyond, these have not generally produced the efficiencies required. The exception has been the production of certain standard fabrics, for example polyester/cotton shirting. But the continual demands of fashion and the resulting changes make any tied system inflexible to the point where commercial viability may be affected. Each stage in the process greatly increases the variety of options available: while there may only be 10 basic fibres there are thousands of different yarns, and so on. For a garment manufacturer, for example, to be tied to one particular fabric source would be to limit impossibly their options. But for that fabric source to produce the variety of fabrics that the garment manufacturer may need in order to meet fashion demands would again be prohibitively expensive. The result is that each stage in manufacture must seek to buy from an ever increasing number of sources to maintain a competitive edge.

Except for the brand new manufacturer or retailer, all parts of the chain have an existing source of supply and an existing market. For continuation of a particular item the first source is that already existing. There must, however, be a continual check of the market to ensure that the price, performance and, indeed, range of aesthetic characteristics such as colours, of the existing supply are competitive with the present market. Change, however, requires a greater market intelligence and for those operating in the forefront of fashion, changing sources can be a continual problem. Information on sources comes from the following main areas:

(1) *Existing suppliers*, who themselves will be sourcing further down the chain and who have the same need to obtain market intelligence. An important customer of a supplier will inevitably be forced to work very closely with them since it is in both their interests to obtain the most up-to-date market information.

(2) *Back selling operations.* All parts of the chain, especially producers of man-made fibres, back sell their products, often leap-frogging fabric and garment manufacturers and liaising directly with the retailer. They may even promote their products directly to the consumer. This marketing operation is backed up with promotions throughout the various stages of the production process, by yarn and fabric development within their own technical departments and by operating a large scale marketing intelligence operation themselves. Fibre producers are often a primary source of information on fashion colours and trends through their support of, and sometimes employment of, specialist consultants in this area.

(3) *Selling activities.* All stages in the process employ representatives who visit a wide variety of potential, if not existing, customers acquainting them with new fabrics etc. This operation is international, carried out either by the company's own representatives based in the overseas country or by agents. These activities, ranging from the casual call to the well-organised visit involving senior executives of both companies, take place on a continual basis.

(4) *Visits to fashion shows and fabric exhibitions.* The international

industry holds a wide variety of fashion, yarn, fabric and garment shows, either organised by itself or through specialist agencies. These may range over the broad spectrum of the market, such as Interstoff in Germany for fabric, or they may be specialist events for one section of the market. Companies send representatives to these exhibitions to meet potential suppliers or to glean information.

(5) *Trade journals.* Articles and advertising features in the wide range of trade journals bring to the attention of buyers and sellers what the market has to offer. These journals often feature articles on fashion shows and exhibitions and again may be general or specialist to one aspect of the trade.

The greatest problem facing the buyer in any section of the market is the plethora of information available. The buyer must on the one hand be receptive to change but on the other must be fully conversant with the potential market. Without a clear understanding of the aesthetic performance and price factors required to meet that market, any sourcing is doomed to failure. Subtleties of colour and styling will be lost in a market which is price orientated only. High standards of performance in certain areas may be totally irrelevant to a fast changing fashion scene.

The decision to buy is not purely dependent on the material alone and its cost, but also on the reliability of supply and the consistency of quality. Such factors mean that large manufacturers or retailers inevitably have more than one supplier for lines which sell in large quantities. An overseas supplier who is cheaper may be backed up by a UK supplier who, even if expensive, is more easily accessible.

Performance

While there are many areas of performance which are important for textile clothing, it is extremely unlikely that all of them will be important for all garments. Their relative importance will vary considerably, not only in terms of garment type but also in terms of the market. In many cases changing performance may have an effect on aesthetics and may increase the cost. The aim should be an optimum level of performance but no more unless this can be achieved without increased cost or harm to aesthetic features.

An extremely difficult area, which will be considered in relation to testing, is what consumers perceive to be a satisfactory quality of performance. The Sale of Goods Act, in stating that goods should be of merchantable quality, in effect lays down only broad guidelines. A shirt clearly must be washable but it does not lay down what the washing conditions should be or a consumer's perceived ideas of what these conditions should be.

Consumers' expectations of performance standard change with time and are influenced by advertising and promotion. Thus, 50 years ago it was acceptable to iron shirts heavily when most of those available were made from cotton without resin treatment. Now consumers are influenced consciously or sub-consciously by the relative ease of ironing easy-care cotton or polyester/cotton shirts and would not accept, in general terms, the level of ironing required by pure cotton.

Consumers are also influenced by what they believe an item should offer them. Thus, an overcoat is expected to keep the wearer warm but a fashion coat is not. Damage to clothing is categorised in the minds of the consumer as their responsibility or the manufacturers' responsibility. This is particularly true in cleaning. Consumers expect to be able to remove certain stains even if they need to use elevated temperatures to do so, but other stains are regarded as the responsibility of the manufacturer. What constitutes heavy wear is very much related to customers' preconceived ideas. This can become a particular issue with children's clothing.

Durability

Durability is often quoted as the most important performance property, although in fact this is often not the case. The difficulty is that durability is extremely complex and very difficult to measure. A clothing item is held together by a complex mixture of physical and chemical forces. Chemical forces bind together the atoms in the basic polymer molecule of the fibre. The fibre itself is held together by inter-molecular forces between the molecules. In a yarn the structure depends on physical force, mainly frictional, between the fibres, induced by laying them parallel and by the application of twist. In a fabric frictional forces between the yarns determine whether the fabric will hold together; if the structure is too loose, slippage of yarn will occur in a woven structure and this may lead to breakdown at seams. Finally, the garment itself is held together by the sewn seam. The durability of a garment is as strong as its weakest point. A very strong fabric may be rendered useless by poor sewing. The difficulty is that different agents will attack different forces within the garment and different conditions of wear will generate those agents.

The commonest physical forces applied to a garment are those of abrasion, tear and lateral strain. Resistance to lateral strain at seams depends on sewing thread and fabric construction; resistance to abrasion depends on fibre strength, i.e. the physical bonds between the molecules and the yarn construction. All these, however, may be to no avail if the fabric is attacked by a chemical agent which destroys the basic fibre molecule. Another agent which seriously degrades fabric is ultra-violet light, generally from sunlight, which again breaks down the molecular structure. This is not usually significant in clothing unless it is worn for highly exposed leisure pursuits but, of course, it becomes very significant in industrial fabrics.

Although durability is often thought of solely in fibre terms, yarn, fabric construction and finishing all play significant roles, and in the garment as a whole the quality of seaming is equally critical. This depends more on the nature of the sewing thread than perhaps the nature of the fabric itself. One example of the complexity of durability is very low twist yarn, spun on a woollen system. This provides such a low level of security in the woven fabric that it may be impossible to sew in inset pockets which require a cut close to the seam corner without that corner fraying out. Another example is a worsted fabric with a very low construction (number of yarns per cm^2). This may result in a cut edge fraying by a centimetre or more before sewing in the conventional sequence. Hence the only way to process such fabrics is to overedge all edges immediately after cutting, which so increases the effective cost of the fabric as to obviate any cost gains in fabric production.

In fibre terms, polyester and nylon are by far the most resistant to physical forces and chemical attack. In resistance to physical forces, wool, silk and even cotton are not a great deal weaker than polyester and nylon but become significantly weaker when the effect of chemical forces is involved. These fibres are severely weakened by agents such as perspiration, alkali detergent and particularly bleach. Acrylic, although much weaker than wool in resistance to physical forces, achieves about the same degree of durability because of its resistance to chemical forces. The regenerated fibres are particularly weak and viscose has the added problem of greatly reduced strength when wet.

In the case of cotton it is important to distinguish between pure cotton and that treated with a resin finish to improve its crease recovery performance. These finishes can result in as much as a 50 per cent drop in durability.

In yarn and fabric construction, higher levels of twist and increased tightness in construction lead to improved durability, although this may increase cost. Worsted spun fabrics are, therefore, generally more durable than woollen spun fabrics, but this must be balanced against the increased thickness of a woollen fabric for a given weight of fibre and hence its better insulation value. The improved durability of polyester over cotton is particularly noticeable in sewing thread; the disintegration of seams at the armhole and the crotch, which happens when cotton threads are used, can be largely avoided if polyester thread is used.

Dimensional stability

Dimensional stability is an important performance characteristic. Since size is a prerequisite for satisfactory purchase, that size must be retained during wear and use if the item is to continue to give customer satisfaction. Despite general belief, none of the commonly used fibres actually shrink on washing although heat can induce shrinkage in some synthetic fibres if they have been incorrectly processed. Wool, as a fibre, does not shrink. What happens is that the naturally occurring scales on the fibres interlock with each other in such a way that agitations cause the item to felt and thus get progressively smaller. Heat and water exacerbate the process and, therefore, washing wool in an untreated form is only possible under extremely mild conditions. This situation can, of course, be avoided by dry cleaning but that is an expensive process and relatively inconvenient; for garments which need frequent cleaning it produces considerable customer resistance. Chemically finished wool sold under the Superwash label enables washing to be safely carried out.

Shrinkage problems, and indeed extension problems which are equally important in terms of size change, do appear in fabrics as a result of incorrect finishing to stabilise strains produced by processing. All fabrics, with the exception of wool already mentioned, can be processed to be perfectly stable in washing conditions. These conditions, however, may not include high temperatures or considerable agitation. The general tendency towards low temperature washing is beneficial in terms of dimensional stability and also in ensuring a retention of other desirable performance properties.

Most fashion garments are required to retain their original appearance as long and under as many varied conditions as possible. It is inevitable that in wear a garment will be creased. If creasing were not possible movement of the arms at the elbows, legs and the knees would be impossible. What matters, therefore, is the recovery from this creasing; in the USA the term 'wrinkle recovery' is often used to describe this. It depends basically on the fibre, and a large number of fibres give reasonable recovery in dry conditions. Unfortunately these conditions are rarely met in wear, due to humidity and of course washing.

Polyester, nylon and resinated cotton give by far the best crease recovery in wet conditions and form the basis of the so-called minimum iron, minimum care, permanent press, etc. type of garment. The names have generally evolved around technical developments but rapidly became marketing concepts in an effort to distinguish one form of treatment from another and suggest to the customer that it had inherent superiority. Silk, viscose unless resin treated, and acetate all give poor crease recovery in the wet.

In a given fibre, finer constructions tend inevitably to have poor crease recovery and knitted structures may absorb creasing better than woven.

In garments, however, there are times when a crease or pleat is required to be durable. The obvious examples are trousers and pleated skirts. Pleats may be set into fabrics using heat or water in the form of steam, or both. For wool, cotton, viscose and silk the changes in structure needed to produce a pleat require water, in the form of steam; in polyester, nylon, acrylic and triacetate they require heat. Because water will allow a crease to be formed the process is easily reversed by washing and hence those fibres are not capable, by simple pressing techniques alone, of taking a durable pleat.

Chemical processes are available for durably pleating wool and the resin finish system on cotton can be adopted to give a durable pleat, but the process adds considerably to the cost of manufacture. With polyester, however, a durable pleat can be obtained at any temperature above about 50°C; it is durable provided subsequent treatments do not exceed that temperature. Thus a pleat in a polyester fabric carried out on a press operating at about 110–150°C would be durable in all normal washing conditions. Durable pleating with heat does, however, limit the washing temperature for polyester fabrics and to ensure that no durable pleating or creasing occurs during washing a temperature of 50°C is not normally exceeded.

Stretch and recovery

In some garment styles stretch is essential for comfort. At points on the human body the skin is required to stretch as much as 50 per cent to accommodate bending and stretching movements, for example at the knees and at the elbows. Any garment which is skin tight would have to stretch this amount under a relatively low load if it was to be considered comfortable. In order to achieve this level of stretch it is essential to use knitted structures, except where a significant percentage of elastane fibre has been incorporated. As the garment becomes looser, the space between the garment and the body allows movement and the need for stretch progressively diminishes. In this way the style of garments has been influenced by considerations of comfort.

Where convention determined that a woven fabric was required for a particular garment, the limitations on stretch which this imposed inevitably meant that the garment had to be cut with a relatively loose fit. Even the advent of elastane fibre, with greater latitude, did not obviate the problem since the high percentage of elastane which would be needed to give stretch at levels of over 50 per cent would be extremely expensive. Textured yarn can also enhance stretch, hence the use of textured nylon knitted hosiery, but on its own this can only marginally improve a woven fabric.

While stretch may be important for comfort, stretch recovery is important to maintain the garment appearance. The stretch available in fibres (except elastane) under reasonable load is far too low to make a significant contribution to the level of stretch and the bulk of stretch comes from the structure. However, in stretching some strain will inevitably be placed on the fibre and the ability of fibre to recover from stretch is therefore critical if bagging or seating is to be avoided. By far the best recovery comes from elastane and nylon. Even polyester does not match up to the recovery of nylon and shows markedly inferior performance in a critical end use such as stockings and tights. Fibres such as cotton and viscose show very poor stretch recovery and consequently have a strong tendency to bag, as for example in denim.

The ultimate performance fabrics in both stretch and stretch recovery are the so-called power nets produced by incorporating high percentages of elastane with nylon in knitted structures; they are used for corsetry and swimwear. Apart from this, aesthetic considerations which determine the choice of fabric may place limitations on closeness of fit if discomfort and bagging are to be avoided.

Pilling and snagging

Pilling and snagging are two surface features regarded as unacceptable in certain garments by customers. Both are features of structure but are affected by the fibre. In the case of pilling, abrasion may rub fibres out of a low twist yarn open structure. Weak fibres tend to rub off but stronger fibres such as polyester tend to remain and the fibres join together to form small balls. Stronger fibres therefore require higher twist in yarns and tighter construction, and they may require special finishing processes, in order to eliminate the pilling problem. The usual sources of the problem are low construction polyester woven fabrics and wool knitwear, the former because of the strength of the fibre and the latter because of the strength of the fibre combined with the low twist open structures generally appropriate to knitwear. Polyester fibres have been produced in so-called low pill varieties and these are suitable for knitwear, but the durability of these fibres is much lower than standard polyester and may even be weaker than wool. Consequently their use in knitwear has been highly restricted and acrylic has generally been favoured.

Snagging results from a knitted structure, or occasionally a woven structure, where a thread is pulled out as a result of contact with a nail or similar protuberance. Care needs to be taken with the structure but in some situations customers may accept responsibility, for example where the snag is caused by a protruding nail or a rose bush. Customer tolerance is also fairly high on stockings and tights.

Moisture absorbency

The moisture absorbency properties of fabrics affect performance in three ways: rate of drying, comfort and static electricity.

When a fabric is wetted moisture is retained within the fibre structure, between the fibres in the yarn and between the yarns in the fabric. The last two, which depend on structure, are relatively easily removed by physical forces such as spin drying, hanging on the line in the wind, wringing or purely by gravity when the garment is hung up. Some structures deliberately exploit this in order to retain moisture, such as the loops in towelling.

The problem, however, of rate of drying results from the tendency of the fibre to absorb water. The broad classification of fibres into hydrophobic (water hating) and hydrophilic (water loving) is too extreme since there is a graduation in moisture absorbancy under normal conditions, from viscose and wool with the highest absorbency, to polyester and polypropylene with the lowest. Cotton tends to be regarded as hydrophilic together with silk, while triacetate and acrylic are regarded as hydrophobic together with nylon.

Essentially, the greater the hydrophobic tendency of the fibre the quicker the fabric will dry or the less heat required to dry it. This has led to the quick-drying, easy-care concept. The increased availability of tumble dryers, although they are expensive to operate, has lessened the importance of this property in the minds of customers, as compared with the 1960s and 1970s. In the case of cotton and viscose, resin treatment markedly reduces water absorbency so that these fibres when resin treated can be regarded as hydrophobic and equivalent to polyester and nylon.

The human body discharges water in the form of perspiration (water vapour) on a continuous basis. The discharge is increased by vigorous exercise and as a means of inducing cooling in hot weather so that it becomes liquid (sweat) rather than vapour. The removal of this perspiration and sweat from the body surface is desirable in terms of hygiene and perceived comfort.

When clothes are being worn the moisture must either escape through openings or pass through the fabric assembly. The first criterion, therefore, for comfort in terms of perspiration removal is sufficient openings on the garment, which is largely a function of style. It is, however, affected by social criteria. The wearing of a tie greatly restricts the opportunity to open a garment at the neck. The fastening of cuffs does likewise. Under these conditions it may be necessary for the perspiration to pass through the fabric assembly. The structure of the fabric will be critical, an open structure obviously allowing easier passage than a tightly constructed one. In this sense knitted fabrics generally have an advantage over woven.

Finally, if passage of perspiration is restricted both in terms of style and fabric structure, then it will be necessary for the perspiration to be absorbed by the fibres and transmitted as in a wick through to the outside. Hydrophilic fibres clearly fulfil this function better than hydrophobic ones – hence the claim that cotton is more comfortable than, say, polyester. It must, however, be noted that when a fibre is saturated the rate of transport of moisture through it is relatively slow and under conditions of extreme heat or, indeed, strenuous exercise a cotton garment will not transmit moisture rapidly enough to avoid discomfort.

Static electricity

Due to friction, all garments generate static charges. These are generally conducted away due to the presence of moisture, and in normal temperate or humid climates this produces no problem. However, under dry conditions such as those experienced in extremely hot or cold climates, there may be insufficient moisture present in the atmosphere to conduct the charge away. Static electricity will, therefore, build up on the garment and will be discharged when the wearer touches a conducting material, quite often metal. The discharge of this current may lead to considerable discomfort but even before that may lead to the garment clinging to the body or, for example, clinging to another garment as in the case of lingerie clinging to a skirt. The increase in static charge may also lead to the attraction of dust particles, thus increasing soiling.

The build up of static charge is less likely in garments containing hydrophilic fibres since these permit discharge due to their retention of moisture. The worst fibres in common use are clearly polyester and nylon and efforts have been made, successfully in the case of nylon, to produce anti-static varieties which greatly reduce this problem. However, it must be stressed that the problem is often overstated since in normal humid conditions discharge takes place immediately. In very dry conditions, however, even cotton and wool can generate static charge, as can be seen if cotton towels are tumble-dried.

The overall result, here, is that the hydrophobic/hydrophilic tendency of fibres favours their performance in one area at the expense of the other. In general terms, the natural fibres have increased comfort but are slow drying, and vice versa with synthetic fibres.

Insulation

In the normal UK situation the weather is such that the human body needs protection to keep warm. Body surface temperature of 37°C is seldom exceeded and in this climate the problem becomes one of insulation to retain heat rather than to exclude it. With exercise the body can metabolise food and generate heat sufficient for comfort to be retained without clothing at temperatures of 25°C and below. People's perception of comfort varies, partly because of metabolic rate. The problem, essentially, is one of restricting heat transfer due to the three causes of conduction, convection and radiation.

The reduction of heat loss by conduction is a function of thickness of an insulating material. The cheapest insulating material is air. Textile fabric essentially acts to trap air, thus providing an insulating media. The fibres have little function other than to prevent the movement of air. The theory is seen at its most graphic in the string vest where air is trapped between the body and outer garment by an open mesh structure. More commonly, garments offering protection from cold conditions use a fibre batt quilted with an outer and inner fabric. The filling may be animal feathers but is more likely to be polyester. The level of quilting is important. The more quilting in terms of decorative effect, the less the effectiveness of conduction since the quilting tends to reduce the thickness of the sewn areas.

At a lower insulation level, techniques such as brushing and raising of the surface, which increase thickness, will increase insulation. The principle has been marketed in thermal underwear and in the thermal garment concept generally. Although superior properties have been claimed for fibres, particularly the chlorofibres, they are not significant because the main insulation comes from the air. Most thermal garments are made from materials with enhanced thickness due to brushing or raising. The old belief in the warmth of wool was related partly to the crimp structure of wool which allowed high bulk fabrics to be produced. Such structures can now, of course, be replicated in synthetic fibres. Hydrophobic fibres have a distinct advantage. Water is a more efficient conductor, and hence a worse insulator, than air. Garments which remain wet are less effective as insulators.

The prevention of heat loss by normal convection is generally carried out by closing the garment at strategic points, such as the cuff, waist and neck, thus preventing the transfer of heat from the warm body to the outside by convected currents. However, a far more serious heat loss is forced convection brought about by the action of the wind. If the wind can penetrate the fabric structure around the body, it will remove heat at a very rapid rate. An impermeable structure is clearly the most desirable but this inhibits perspiration loss and therefore produces discomfort. Fabric coatings are now available which give a microporous structure that allows some passage of water vapour but minimises the passage of wind (and outside water). In general terms, knitted structures which are more open permit the passage of wind more easily, and a knitted sweater, while giving excellent insulation from conducted heat loss, may be quite useless in windy conditions.

The third heat loss, radiation, becomes more significant at lower temperatures. These are normally only encountered in leisure activities such as mountain climbing and hill walking. The radiated heat can be reflected back using a shiny surface, usually aluminium foil, laminated to the wadding in an anorak structure. This foil may be microporous in order to permit perspiration loss.

In fashion garments worn primarily indoors, the question of insulation simply does not arise. The ambient temperature is sufficient to prevent discomfort. Indeed, thin fabrics may be necessary to prevent discomfort from overheating.

Protection from rain

Some clothing is designed to protect the wearer from outside water, particularly rain. The structures of woven and knitted fibres are sufficiently porous to allow the easy passage of water regardless of hydrophobic or hydrophilic tendency. The only truly waterproof finish is a continuous coating, usually of polyvinyl or polyurethane. The substrate is usually polyester or nylon. However, this removes the aesthetic characteristics of the textile fibre and creates problems of permeability to allow loss of perspiration.

The so-called raincoat has been used for a number of years as a compromise. Here the fabric is finished with a silicone which increases the surface tension between the fabric surface and water, thus encouraging water to form droplets which run off. There is a limit to the size of the pore that can be protected in this way and in general only woven fabrics of a reasonably tight construction are likely to be successful. Even here the finish is not waterproof, it is only resistant to rain. Unfortunately this raises the question of the intensity of the rain and even such terms as 'shower resistant' are now generally avoided because they raise questions of what constitutes a shower. While this method of fabric treatment definitely has beneficial results, it has a generally low credibility among consumers because of poor standards in the past. Consequently claims based on proofed fabrics are often adversely scrutinised by Trading Standards Officers. This is unfortunate because the garment does offer a compromise between porosity, comfort and water repellency.

Dye-fastness

One of the commonest causes of complaint about garments is loss of colour both during wear and particularly during cleaning. The bonding between the dye-stuff molecule and a fibre generally involves physical forces. Chemical bonding does not take place except in the case of reactive dyes on cotton and viscose. Dyes are not therefore permanently fast to all conditions. Even if they were, there would be the problem of ultra-violet light, mainly from sunlight, which destroys dye molecules and so causes colours to fade. Customers have tended to accept a level of colour change and, indeed, may not even perceive it if the fading takes place uniformly over a long period of time. However, if the colour loss is gross and if the colour stains on to other materials, either when being worn or in cleaning, complaints are inevitable.

Although dye-fastness to perspiration can be tested, commercial dye-stuffs available from most manufacturers do not significantly deteriorate, although testing for rubbing is important. A great many dye-stuff problems result not from an inherent incompatibility between the dye-stuff and the fabric but rather because incorrect conditions have been used for a particular batch. One problem is surplus dye not being cleared from the fabric after processing and it may lie on the surface and rub off during wear either on to the individual or on to their clothing. All dyes eventually fade under light but for fashion garments this may not be significant. It may, however, cause problems in garments such as swimwear which are by their nature exposed to a high level of sunlight. Similar special conditions apply to exposure to salt water and particularly to chlorinated water; swimwear, again, is particularly susceptible.

The main problem with dye-stuffs almost inevitably comes during cleaning, and particularly washing. Since most dyes are deposited from aqueous solution or suspension they are more easily removed by water than by dry cleaning. There is a tendency therefore for suppliers to mark garments 'dry clean only' and thus, they believe, obviate any problems. In fact problems may still occur, although not as frequently, but except for certain high fashion, rarely worn items, the *necessity* as opposed to the *possibility* of dry cleaning forms a real deterrent to consumer purchase.

In practice, the majority of colours on the majority of fabrics can be dyed perfectly satisfactorily and be fast for washing provided the correct conditions are used. There are likely to be two problems: the actual removal of the dye-stuff, causing a change in colour, and the staining off of the dye-stuff on to adjacent materials in the wash. To overcome the latter it is quite common to use designations like 'wash separately' or even 'hand wash'. All these, however, are deterrents to consumer acceptance. The consumer might accept 'wash separately' for a large bulky item such as a raincoat, but certainly would not accept it for a small item of underwear. The temperature of washing is critical. The higher the temperature the more likely the dye is to be removed. Again, the tendency towards low temperature washing greatly improves the prospects for consumer satisfaction in dye fastness.

Flame retardancy

The problem of fire-resistance or flame retardancy continues to excite some consumer interest, especially in household furnishings, but occasionally too in everyday clothing. The problem is that the only fibres which will not burn – i.e. do not react with the oxygen in the air, generating heat – are glass and asbestos. Neither of these merit consideration for clothing. Provided there is a sufficient heat source, generally over 300°C, all common fibres will burn. What distinguishes them is whether that burning is self-sustaining after the source of fire has been removed. The cellulose-based fibres such as cotton and viscose continue to burn at a rapid rate. The process is exacerbated by the design of garments. A light party dress with layers of cotton petticoats underneath ensures an adequate supply of oxygen for the burning process and hence the maximum rate of burning. It was for this reason that such garments were banned for children.

Acrylic, acetate and triacetate also continue to burn but not at the rate of cotton and viscose. Polyester and nylon generally extinguish themselves because the process of burning melts the fibre in advance of the flame and the molten polymer tends to self-extinguish. However, if either is blended with as little as 30 per cent of cotton or viscose the flame is self-progagating. Wool and silk rapidly extinguish but the best fibre in terms of non-propagation is modacrylic. This is a modification to acrylic fibres which is generally not favoured for garments such as knitwear because of its slightly less acceptable handle and higher price. However, it is used for certain items of children's wear such as dressing gowns, as well as for some items of household furnishing.

Flame retardant finishes are available for cotton and other cellulose fibres, mainly based on phosphorus compounds. These have problems of durability and adversely affect the handle as perceived by the customer. They are, however, used on certain items of workwear. High flame resistant versions of nylon are also available, which find such specialised uses as racing drivers' overalls, but it must be accepted that the public is not generally concerned with flame retardancy as part of their normal everyday clothing. Whether increased awareness will result from consumer pressure groups or from some accident which receives considerable media attention remains to be seen, but the current trend towards natural fibres, particularly cotton, in pure untreated form hardly makes it easy to achieve any flame retardant objective.

From time to time technological developments claiming to improve performance are promoted to the consumer. Examples in the past have been moth repellent finishes, largely now confined to the treatment of carpets, soil removal or resistant finishes, anti-bacterial finishes to eliminate odours etc. The value of any finish will vary and may be susceptible to cleaning processes. The problem is always that the advantages, as perceived by the customer, may ultimately be outweighed by disadvantage. This may be price but could also be an effect on other performance properties or aesthetics. While certain performance factors are built in to the consumer acceptance of textile items, others are transitory and are important only as long as publicity remains.

Testing

The most obvious way to test clothing for performance factors would appear to be a wearer or user trial. Under certain circumstances such tests are essential but, as a routine form of investigation, they have inherent problems. First, they may be time consuming. Properties such as durability may take months to investigate. Secondly, wearer variability is a considerable problem. For the trial to be statistically viable a large number of garments may have to be issued and problems then arise over controlling wearers and getting the information back. All this can be expensive and time consuming. So laboratory testing has to be relied on to provide a picture, coupled with known technological facts about fibres and fabric performance. For a laboratory test of a performance factor to be viable it must satisfy the following:

(1) It must replicate as closely as possible the actual conditions of wear and use. In some cases this is relatively easy. Washing, for example, can easily be replicated by using a washing machine and this can allow for dimensional stability and colour fastness testing. Other properties are much less easily simulated, such as durability where only certain aspects, normally physical, can be accounted for.

(2) The test must be reproducible. Standard pieces of test equipment which can give consistent results are therefore required. These need to be set up in a laboratory which may require standard conditions such as controlled temperature and humidity.

(3) The test must be capable of yielding quantitative data. This could be relatively straightforward, like the loading required to tear a

fabric of a standard width pulled at a standard rate, or it could mean setting up an artificial, but 'nonetheless internationally accepted, scale, like the grey scale for assessing colour change and staining on fabrics.

(4) There must be a means of correlating the results with actual practice. Clearly the more closely the test reproduces actual wear and use conditions, the more likely there is to be correlation, although in several important properties, such as durability, correlation is extremely difficult. The process of refining test methods and modifying standards in the light of experience is continuous in the performance evaluation of textiles.

In terms of the performance factors set out earlier in this chapter the following generally applies to laboratory testing.

Durability

Durability testing is almost entirely related to physical forces acting on fabrics. It can give good correlatable results for seam breakage and seam slippage, for example, and reasonable correlation in some other areas of durability, particularly for fabrics with particular weaknesses such as resinated cotton. However, there is a tendency to assume that the use of synthetic fibres such as polyester and nylon will guarantee durability, and while this is sometimes a mistake because of the influence of construction, it has some basis in that both these fibres provide adequate protection from chemical attack. The main testers used are the Instron, or similar tenacity strength tester, the Martindale abrasion tester, and to a limited extent the Elmendorf tear strength tester.

Dimensional stability

Dimensional stability can be relatively easily checked. The biggest problems occur in use, particularly cleaning, but it must be remembered that dimensional stability is also critical during the making up process. Standardised test equipment, such as the Wascator machine, is used in testing laboratories but a close approximation can be given in any normal domestic washing machine.

Crease recovery

Testers exist to measure crease recovery, such as the Shirley crease recovery tester, but these are seldom used except on a quality control basis. If specific claims are being made for easy-iron performance the usual method is to subject a sample to washing and observe its appearance. A scale operating from 1 to 5, known as the Monsanto scale, is sometimes used to grade this performance. If easy care performance is required the usual method is to select on the basis of fibres.

To test for pleat retention, the usual method is to make a pleat in a piece of sample material and subject it to a cleaning treatment.

Stretch and recovery

Testing for stretch and recovery can be carried out on load application machines of the Instron type. These are frequently used where particular claims are being made and where the end use is specifically related to stretch, as in swimwear. In other cases shape retention is based around the use of fibres or on structures which give the necessary stretch, mainly knitted.

Pilling and snagging

Specific test methods exist for pilling and snagging, mainly the ICI pillbox tester, the Mace snagging tester and the Atlas pill tester. Correlation of these results in practice is difficult and requires expert knowledge, but the sensitivity of customers to a high level of pilling on certain garments makes some sort of test method essential.

Moisture absorption

No specific test for moisture absorption is normally carried out. If this is a factor reliance is placed on the known properties of fibres.

Insulation

For insulation properties, test methods which give results in terms of 'togs' are available. This is only a measure of conduction. The results are frequently quoted for duvets and sleeping bags but not generally for clothing.

Water proofing

The two most widely used methods for rain proof or water proof testing are the Bundesmann and the Credit rain simulators. Both give measures of water penetration and absorption but the difficulty is always in correlating the level of water dropped on to the fabric with rain in real life. Nevertheless, they are used as a guide when any claim for shower or rain resistance is being made.

Colour fastness

Tests for colour fastness are well developed. Those for rubbing (Crockmeter), perspiration and washing correlate well with use and employ the standard grey scales operating in the range 1 to 5 for both change of shade and staining. Light fastness testing is also extensively carried out, principally using the Xenon Arc, but again the correlation with real life is difficult. However, an experienced operator can give a reasonable guide.

Laboratory testing

Laboratory testing is extensive for flame resistance, using equipment operating to British Standards. This measures the rate of propagation or otherwise of a flame which is applied in a standard form for a set period of time. Although mainly used on furnishings because of recent legislation, the equipment is used on clothing, particularly children's wear.

Laboratory tests

Laboratory tests for textiles are invaluable despite the difficulties of correlation in many areas. They are used for predicting behaviour in order to produce an acceptable product, and for routine quality control. The tests considered above relate principally to clothing but, of course, testing is required at all stages of manufacture from fibre through yarn to fabric, to ascertain suitabilities for the next stage of the process. Extensive laboratory test methods exist to evaluate the strength of fibres and other properties related to their ability to spin, to evaluate yarns both for strength and evenness and their ability to be woven or knitted, and for control in the wide variety of dyeing and finishing processes.

Testing is also required by the garment maker to ensure that the final product meets customer satisfaction and that the fabric and trimmings can be used in garment manufacture satisfactorily. Some of the properties tested, such as dimensional stability and colour fastness, will be the same as those for finished clothing but the test methods will differ because they will be required to simulate making up conditions rather than wearing conditions. Thus for dimensional stability it is important that no change of size occurs during pressing, fusing and other operations, so the test methods will be adjusted accordingly.

A particular property of concern to some sections of clothing manufacture is the ability of the fabric to mould or shape. This property is sometimes called 'formability', based on work carried out in Sweden in the 1960s.

A further aspect of testing is the control of what could be termed 'aesthetic properties': handle, drape, flexibility, etc. Since these characteristics are important in customer acceptance of a garment, the ability to control them and, in particular, the ability to ensure that successive deliveries have the same characteristics, are extremely important. A number of test methods seek to quantify these properties, such as the Shirley stiffness tester and the Cusick drape tester. Recently an extensive system of fabric testing, known as the Kawabata system, has been introduced. This is capable of a detailed examination of aesthetic properties and relates them to formability. Interpretation of results is complex but the equipment is being increasingly used as a quality control measure and, by establishing desirable properties in making up terms and handle, as a means of assessing fabrics for purchase.

Specifications

As laboratory tests must conform to certain criteria in order to give a reproducible quantitative result, what matters ultimately is not the result but whether it is acceptable or not. The basis of acceptability must be the end use, that is the garment which is being sold and the market into which it is being sold. The criteria of acceptance in terms of performance for a school anorak for the mid-market are substantially different from those for a fashion dress for the up-market.

The first decision is to determine what performance properties are significant. These may then be accounted for in terms of fibre or fabric construction before a decision is made on what test results need to be known in order to determine satisfaction. Performance properties which must be evaluated by a test method before material can be accepted for end use form the basis of a specification. This needs to stipulate the performance property being evaluated and the actual test method used, together with the level of quantitative value which will be acceptable. This is critical. If the standard accepted is too low, customer dissatisfaction will result; if it is too high, fabrics or trimmings may be rejected unnecessarily, making it difficult to achieve the aesthetic requirements or greatly increasing the cost. Almost worse than no standards at all are standards which are set impossibly high.

A specification needs to be drawn up for each stage of the process, but its ultimate aim should be to generate the ability to meet the specification for the ultimate end use. Performance difficulties in the garment frequently result from failure to meet any form of specification during yarn processing which, for example, results in pilling. In some organisations this level of control operates in the whole manufacturing process, frequently controlled by the ultimate retailer. However, this may not always be possible and garment manufacturers and retailers may have to rely on testing which begins at the fabric stage only.

For many garments the specification is not long or complex. Indeed, dimensional stability, colour fastness and a simple strength test may be all that is required. These, however, make all the difference between customer dissatisfaction and satisfaction. Specifications must accord with any claims or cleaning instructions being made about the garment. Testing may be used to determine what washing instructions are included, or a decision may be made about the minimum cleaning requirements that can be accepted, and this is incorporated in the criteria of acceptance for a particular property. Thus, if it is decided as a matter of policy that a garment must be machine washable but that it is not likely to encounter heavy soiling and could be machine washed satisfactorily at 40°C, then an appropriate test with an acceptable dimensional stability and colour fastness level would be incorporated in the specification. On the other hand, if it had been determined that a particular fabric had such a high fashion appeal that it was going to be used in any event, the test procedure could determine whether it was labelled washable or dry clean only.

The lack of a simple specification of criteria for acceptance for important performance properties is the biggest single cause of ultimate customer dissatisfaction in the clothing industry. The effect may be felt directly in terms of returned garments, which may run into thousands, or indirectly in a fall off in sales.

Developments

The clothing industry has existed and reached its present volume of business by encouraging the concept of change. Customers are encouraged to buy clothing over and above their needs by the inducements of fashion and technological advance. In the period between 1955 and about 1975 substantial technological developments were introduced to the industry, notably the range of synthetic fibres. These had a major impact and in themselves generated consumer demand for change. During this period and subsequently, changes in fashion to meet lifestyles have been a constant impetus and, since the pace of technological change has slowed down, have been the most important factor in sustaining the level of demand. There can be little doubt that even if there is 'nothing new in fashion', changing requirements of fashion over a limited period will continue to provide the impetus for change. The question is whether there will be technological developments to contribute to this process.

It would be extremely foolish to be dogmatic in prediction but it would seem unlikely that technological change will take place on the scale that operated between 1955 and 1975.

The cost of developing and promoting a new fibre, against the world economic situation, appears to be prohibitive. The synthetic fibres which have been developed complement well the properties of natural fibres and have reached established positions. While there will be manoeuvring for market share and changes in the relative balance between the fibres, it would appear that the number of common commercially available fibres is likely to reduce rather than increase, although variations on synthetic fibres of the so-called second and third order variety – to introduce, for example, improved dye up-take – will certainly occur. In yarn production, improvements aimed at productivity in spinning methods will continue and it appears likely that the dominant position of false twisting as a texturising method will be challenged.

Weaving and knitting are likely to remain the basic methods of producing fabric. The most interesting developments are likely to come in the continuing attempts to provide non-wovens which have acceptable aesthetic characteristics for clothing. If this is achieved and making up methods can be adopted accordingly, the possibility of disposable garments will again become important in the general clothing sector as opposed to the specialised industrial area where they are now dominant. Such a concept does not obviate the need for performance testing; it simply means that the criteria of acceptance are changed. Even a disposable garment has to last some period of time and if it does not, as happened with many of those sold in the early 1970s, customers will be dissatisfied. Nevertheless, the disposable concept has continued to grow.

The 1980s have seen the replacement of woven textile fabrics in nappies. Disposable fabric now almost has a monopoly for graduation gowns in the USA. The next most obvious opportunity in garments worn for only one day is wedding gowns, although the marketing and technological barriers here may be insuperable.

Developments in dyeing and finishing techniques and the possibility of new finishes are highly likely. Work continues on developing a finish for cotton which will enhance its easy care properties but not at the expense of durability. A similar finish may yet be developed for silk. Finishes will be particularly aimed at enabling natural fibres to regain the market share they lost to synthetics.

The greatest changes may come in garment manufacture. The problem is still, essentially, the difficulty in developing a robotic system capable of handling a limp flexible fabric. The basic joining method remains the sewing machine and despite improvements on the fringe, the basic handling method is still human. In the longer term the solution may be to turn away from the cut pattern joined together by seaming, to the principle of moulding to obtain shape, thus reducing to a minimum the joining operation. Such a change, however, would require enormous changes in customers' aesthetic acceptances and while this may not be a problem in industrial garments it might be considerably different in the general market.

Although the future is likely to be one of evolution rather than revolution, it must be remembered that the clothing industry is not isolated; it is subject to the influence of developments in other areas, particularly in cleaning techniques. Developments in detergents, such as more effectiveness at lower temperatures, will have a considerable effect on performance requirements, as great as those brought about by the original widespread introduction of washing machines. But, above all, it will be changes in consumer lifestyle which will affect the demands on the industry. The ever-increasing trend towards more leisure activity but with associated active forms of leisure pursuits, is likely to lead to the development of clothing specifically designed for activities which could require performance specifications currently not considered viable. An obvious area is in insulation and weather-proofing.

Compromises in practice

This chapter has summarised the processes of fabric manufacture against the background of the compromises needed in aesthetics, performance and price, in the search for the right fabrics to incorporate in marketable garments.

One example of such a compromise lies in the development of 'drip dry', non-iron shirts. The first phase attempted to maintain the aesthetic properties of pure cotton and provided a non-iron finish by resinating the fabric. This was aesthetically successful but performance in wear was poor because the fibres degraded rapidly at neck and cuffs. The compromise later achieved was the development of a range of shirting fabrics containing a mixture of polyester and cotton, giving a satisfactory non-iron performance but not maintaining fully the handle and drape of pure cotton. Nylon in a knitted fabric gives the best performance, in terms of wear and non-iron properties, but its aesthetic properties are no longer acceptable and it has the additional disadvantage of providing a poor micro-climate for the wearer owing to its low absorbency, lack of wicking power and low 'breathability'.

The above example illustrates a compromise achieved by selecting appropriate fibres. Another common compromise balances aesthetics against price; in other words an attempt to maintain the image of a high price fabric while using a lower priced alternative to serve a larger market. An obvious example is to copy a silk wedding dress in a polyester fabric. The handle of 100 per cent pure, virgin wool can be simulated at a lower price by an admixture of previously used fibre. In a different field, the classic method of producing check fabric is by weaving an appropriate series of coloured yarns in both warp and weft. A much more economical method, used in fabrics for children's garments and lower priced blouses and dresses, is to weave or knit a plain fabric and print the checks on to it.

A third sort of compromise is between performance and price. For instance, within a given range of fabrics wearing qualities relate, among other factors, to the amount of twist in the yarns and the density of warp and weft threads. Lower twist and fewer threads is cheaper but performs less well; higher twist and more threads is dearer and performs better. The particular point in the range which the designer selects is a matter of that designer's judgement of what the market will accept – both in performance and price.

Finally, it is wise to remember what may be called 'anti-compromise', arising from the factor with which the whole fabric and clothing industry is riddled: 'perceived value'. Woven 100 per cent cashmere bears a high price and a high cachet, but its performance properties are marred by its low wearing qualities, its easy distortion and the difficulty of inserting cut-through pockets. Similarly a 100 per cent silk suit is highly priced, but the wearer cannot sit down in either trousers or skirt without extensive creasing. It is salutary to recall the Swedish rainwear manufacturer whose designer produced a ladies' proofed silk raincoat in the 1960s. The company marketed this design on a small scale and tentatively, but was for some years overwhelmed with demand from retailers throughout Europe, in spite of its relatively poor performance and high price. The market's high perceived value for this product kept sales high.

6

Manufacture

Stated very simply, clothing manufacture consists of cutting, sewing, fusing, a few alternative methods of joining fabrics, and pressing. Cutting breaks down into marker making, spreading and cutting. Apart from marker making, dealt with in Chapter 7, the decisions of the designer do not directly influence the technology and methods of the cutting room.

The principles of garment construction concern the assembly of fabric parts to make a garment, the addition of working parts to enable the wearer to put on and take off the garment, the decoration of the garment by stitching on the surface of the fabric, the lining and interlining of the garment, and the insertion of pockets whether decorative or functional. For the purposes of crude classification, it may be useful to consider garments as a system of irregular tubes. A trouser is two tubes joined together at fork, fly and seat, a jacket is three tubes joined together at the armholes, a dress is three tubes and a skirt is one tube. Some tubes, such as a jacket, are not completely closed; indeed a tabard is merely two pieces of fabric joined by ties at the side. A typical tube is joined longitudinally by seams, finished at the bottom or hem, and finished at the top usually in a much more elaborate and eye-catching way.

Garment assembly

As with many products assembled from components, much of the technique of garment construction is designed to ensure the continuous, finished appearance of the product. Since fabric edges are often rough and unfinished and fray easily, they must be turned inside the garment. In order to sew a simple seam, the edges of two components are positioned face to face, stitched together continuously, and opened so that the face of the fabric is on the outside of the garment and the two edges of the seam on the inside. British Standard 3870: Part 2: 1983 lists 284 seam types (many with subdivisions), some of which are edge finishing rather than strictly joining, and there are other conformations of seams not included in the standard.

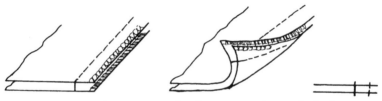

Fig. 6.1 'Plain seam' with edges separately overlocked.

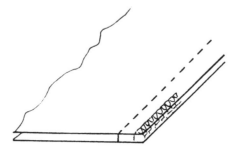

Fig. 6.2 'Plain seam' with edges overlocked together.

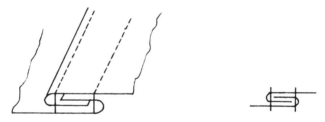

Fig. 6.3 Lap felled seam.

The 'plain' seam (Fig. 6.1) is most frequently used in closing two edges of woven cloths. The two raw edges are first overlocked separately, then the seam is sewn and finally pressed open. Alternatively, the two raw edges are overlocked together at the same time as the seam is closed (Fig. 6.2). In this case the seam cannot be pressed open but the two seam edges are pressed to one side inside the garment, with the seam on the outside showing a slight ridge at the join. The first type consumes more time but produces a better finish and is very common in the seams of trousers, skirts and jackets. The second type is quicker, because all the sewing is done simultaneously, but produces a slightly less acceptable finish and is found, for instance, in the seams of boys' trousers and lower priced women's trousers.

Much more common on the long seams of jeans and shirts is the so-called lap felled seam, sewn with two rows of stitching on a twin needle machine (Fig. 6.3). This provides a very strong seam in garments that will take a lot of wear.

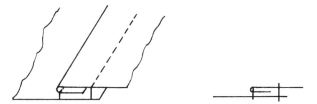

Fig. 6.4 Welted or raised seam.

The type of raised, top stitched seam often used on skirt panel seams, trouser side seams and overcoat seams is also technically a lapped seam, but is often referred to as a welted seam or a raised seam (Fig. 6.4).

These examples only introduce the subject of seaming. Much more information will be found in Carr and Latham, *The Technology of Clothing Manufacture* and in British Standard 3870: Part 2: 1983.

The properties of seams combine standards of appearance and performance with economy. Good appearance usually means smooth joining with no uneven stitches, no wrinkles, no pucker and no fullness. Sometimes the designer will specify regular gathering or a controlled amount of ease or fullness to ensure a good fit.

Performance of seams means strength, elasticity, durability, security and comfort, plus specialised objectives such as the waterproofing of some rainwear seams and the flameproofing of seams in children's nightdresses (a legal requirement). Manufacturers aim to make the seam as strong as the fabric, both parallel to and at right angles to the seam. Seams must also stretch and recover with the fabric, especially when in some swimwear up to 100 per cent stretch is required. Seams must also be durable to the abrasion of wear and washing and secure from the unravelling of stitches. A seam in a close fitting garment must not present a noticeable ridge or roughness to the skin (the same applies to manufacturer's brand labels, a cause of concern for some time).

This issue of economy arises because many seams can be constructed in a number of ways. Many of the more complex machines and stitch types allow short cuts to be taken, but both appearance and performance may vary. The end use of the garment and its price level both influence the decision on seaming methods.

Hemming

Apart from two exceptions, an overcoat made of naval melton and a knitted garment, some work must be performed during assembly to

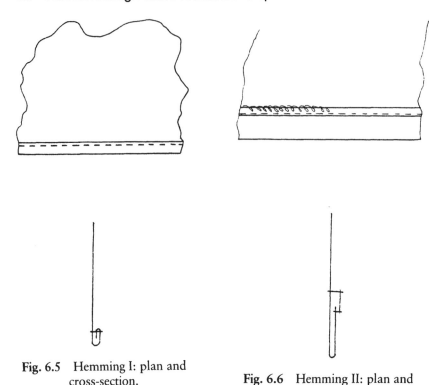

Fig. 6.5 Hemming I: plan and cross-section.

Fig. 6.6 Hemming II: plan and cross-section.

finish the bottom of a garment. One method is to turn over the edge twice, thus enclosing the raw edge, and sew the inner turned edge to the outer fabric by two thread lockstitch, as in some shirts, or by blindstitch, as in some part-lined jackets (Fig. 6.5). Alternatively the raw edge of the fabric may be finished by overlocking, or covered by tape, turned up and secured by blindstitch (Fig. 6.6).

In a lined garment, the lining may be sewn to the edge of the turnup, thus covering the raw edge. In addition the lining of a sleeve usually plays a part in holding the cuff turnup in position, because the lining itself is fastened to the sleeve seam. In the bottom of a jacket the cloth turnup is secured independently by blindstitch.

Closing the top

When the garment hangs from the waist, such as a trouser or skirt, the work content involved in finishing the top is usually much greater than the bottom, because it has to fit the waist and provide fashion interest. One of the simplest methods of finishing the waist, sometimes used in skirt making, covers the raw edge of the fabric with a woven laterally stiff tape (petersham) and turns over the top edge by pressing. The raw edge of the top may alternatively be fastened to woven elastic, as with men's briefs, or turned over to form a tunnel with elastic through it, or the elastic may be held in position with multiple rows of stitching, as is more usual with pyjamas.

More commonly, outer garments carry a separate waistband, cut along the length of the fabric to gain the advantage of the relative stability of the warp. The waistband may be relatively narrow, turned over once on an interlining, the edge overlocked or taped, and held in position by stitching through from the outside close to the band seam. Alternatively, instead of being turned over the interlining, the cloth band is sometimes faced with a lining which carries a soft canvas backing. The lining itself may be in simple form with the bottom raw edge turned up behind its canvas backing so that when the lining is secured by stitching through from the outside, this raw edge finishes inside. Another type of band lining is fastened by blindstitch or by hand to the pockets of the trouser. It is sewn to the band with slight fullness and is constructed with pleats to create extra length along the bottom edge. The circumference of the trouser when worn is slightly longer than at the top of the band, and such a lining will be snug inside the trouser and will not tend to curl up.

When the garment hangs from the shoulders the closing of the top involves shoulder, collars and armholes and can vary in complexity from a dress without collar or sleeves to a jacket with both. Shirt construction includes a back yoke and shoulders with safety stitching or lap felled seams, and a collar which may comprise up to 40 per cent of total work content of the shirt. Dress construction includes closing the shoulder seams with plain seams, pressed open, or French seams, or safety stitch seams in knitted fabric; and sewing facings, with edges secured perhaps by overlocking, to armholes and neck opening, with sometimes a soft tape to stabilise the shape.

In a suit jacket, shoulder seams are usually designed to curve forward to the shoulder point. The back shoulder is longer than the front and fullness is created in about the centre half of the seam. The prime difficulty in assembling a collar to a jacket lies in applying the two dimensions of the fabric to the three dimensions of the finished collar. Both the leaf edge and the stand edge of the collar need to be longer than the crease edge, so it is necessary to use a soft melton cut on the bias as an undercollar. This is not necessary on overcoats, because the softer fabrics more usual in these garments allow the required manipulation. The undercollar is sewn on to the neck and pressed into position. In the past, before covering the undercollar with the top collar it was stretched at both the leaf and stand edges. A more logical approach is the split collar (Fig. 6.7). Here the stand is a separate piece of fabric which is sewn to the fall in such a way that the

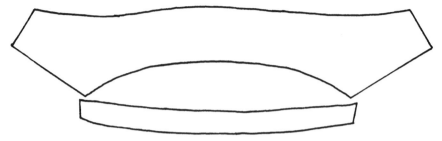

Fig. 6.7 Split collar.

seam comes just inside the collar crease. Pattern construction provides the requisite length for both stand and fall.

The armhole is prepared to receive the sleeve around all but the top front of the crown. The back is slightly drawn in. The sleeve is sewn in with fullness over the crown, tailing off below the side seam, and with sufficient fullness at the front pitch to prevent any break in the front drape of the sleeve. The chest piece, already carrying the shoulder pad, is fastened to the armhole seam in such a manner that there is a slight horizontal ease between the gorge and the front armhole, keeping the outer fabric taut and inducing a slight hollow in the garment.

Lining

The inside of a garment must present a finished appearance. If a garment such as a blouse or dress has no lining, the customer expects the inside to be clean with seams that will not degrade during washing. The purposes of a lining are to cover and protect the seams inside a garment, to provide an aesthetically appealing inside surface, and to present a sheer surface to other garments so that the lined garment is easy to put on and take off. Hence the fabric used is commonly viscose or acetate rayon or woven nylon.

The assembly of the lining itself follows the same pattern as the assembly of the outer fabric. The seams are almost always plain seams, not usually pressed open but with both seam inlays pressed to one side to prevent the slight appearance of seam grin which would otherwise result on the sheer fabric of linings.

When a lining is no more than an aesthetic cover for the inside of a garment, it must fit the outer fabric form in such a way that not only does it avoid disturbing the designed outward appearance but it must also itself appear clean and finished. In other words it must be slightly longer in all dimensions, without actually appearing to be so, and where the garment outer cloth stretches and relaxes to the movement of the wearer the lining must also move in the same way. For instance, the back of a jacket lining usually carries a vertical pleat to allow lateral movement of the fabric. Alternatively, lining can have a function as well as an aesthetic appeal in skirts and trousers. Where the outer fabric might be unstable in wear, the function of the lining is to assist, by its stability, in preserving the designed shape of the garment. Tweed trousers and skirts should be lined. A final objective of lining is to provide a backing for see-through cloths in lower garments.

The finishing of the bottom of a lining follows the same principles as those of the outer cloth. In a free lining the bottom can be turned over twice and secured by two thread lockstitch. It may be fastened to the bottom of the cloth of, say, a topcoat by a few chains of thread 3–5 cm long. Alternatively, on a close fitting trouser leg the bottom of the lining is acceptable when simply pinked. When the lining is closed to the bottom of the cloth the 'bellows' bottom is almost invariable. This is simply a horizontal pleat to allow vertical movement in the outer fabric.

In the fitting of a lining to a jacket, the assembly of the front edges is important because the facing is usually of the same fabric as the outer cloth. Extra fabric is needed vertically to prevent a break at the base of the lapel, and horizontal fullness is needed to allow for the curl of the lapel. The front edge is stayed, by tapes of considerable variety, to control the front edge of the garment. Without this control the garment might show unsightly fluting. It is also necessary to prevent the facing rolling outside the front edge below the lapel, and to prevent the front rolling outside the facing on the lapel. This is achieved sometimes by chainstitch basting the edge and subsequent pressing, or by securing inside the front edge with a specialised form of blindstitch called 'bluffing', or externally by one of several forms of edge stitching. The rear edge of the fabric facing is fastened to the chest piece and the pocket bag.

Interlining

Modern Western civilisation requires outer garments to streamline the body of the wearer. The human body bends forwards at the waist, and human beings communicate face to face. These two factors demand the streamlining and reinforcing of the front of clothing. The addition of interlining to a garment not only reinforces the outer fabric but adds resilience to it so that when a person stands upright the front of the garment returns to its former shape without wrinkles or creasing. Other areas which may call for reinforcement are collars, cuffs and waistbands.

Almost universally nowadays, interlinings are fusible. They consist of a base cloth, which may be similar to those used for non-fusible interlinings, which carries a thermoplastic adhesive resin which will melt when heated to a specific temperature. If it is laid flat on to a garment part and heat and pressure are applied, the resin will flow into the fabric of the garment and it and the interlining will become permanently attached. This laminate will then be handled as one piece of material. There may always be places where sew-in interlinings have to be used, but in the vast majority of volume garment production fusing is the accepted method.

The advantages of using a fusible interlining are largely economic. In most cases the use of fusibles shortens manufacturing time, especially in large area applications such as all kinds of coat fronts. Less skill and therefore less training time are required to carry out most fusing operations. It is easier to achieve consistent quality in the laminating process than with sewn-in interlinings. It might still be claimed that, in individual cases, a craftsman using traditional canvas interlining can produce garments with a subtlety of contour, a softness and a crease recovery that fusing cannot, but the overall cost of manufacturing by this method is enough to be uncompetitive for all but a few people.

The designer chooses fusible interlinings to fulfil the requirements of appearance and performance throughout the life of the garment. The laminate produced by fusing should show the aesthetic qualities required by the designer in the finished garment, in particular the flexibility or draping qualities of the garment. Achieving the required stiffness, handle or draping qualities is not always predictable from the properties of the two plies of the laminate, and is a matter of trial and error before manufacturing begins. The designer may choose the drape of the fusible's base cloth and the type and quantity of the fusible resin forming the bond. In the search for a softer handle, the choice may be a compromise between the strength of the bond, as measured by standard tests, and those qualities referred to as stiffness, handle and drape, based on a subjective judgement. A laminate will normally show crease recovery properties somewhere between the better component and the worst, and it may vary with the grain direction of the fabric.

The strength of the bond in the laminate must be sufficient to withstand handling during subsequent operations, the flexing which takes place in wear, the temperature and agitation of a washing and drying cycle, or the solvents, temperature and agitation of a dry-cleaning process (and in some cases both). If there is not a complete and even bond over the whole surface of the laminate when first fused, or if delamination takes place at some stage in the garment's life, it will appear as a bubbling in the outer fabric of the garment. Parts which appear to be satisfactorily fused initially could have a bond which is below the required strength. The likelihood of future failure cannot be discovered by eye or handle, but must be eliminated and controlled by enforcing a rigorous testing procedure, applied to the temperature, the pressure and the time cycle of the fusing press and also to the product of the press, both test pieces and whole garments. Possible defects of the process must be avoided: strike-through or strike-back (fusible resin showing through on either side of the laminate), dye sublimation, thermal shrinkage of the outer fabric or the crushing of high pile fabric.

Functional parts

If garments are designed to fit the body it would be impossible to get in or out of them, in many cases, without the insertion of working parts to open or close them. Many designers enhance these parts in order to make them features in the design.

The commonest of these are buttons and buttonholes. Buttons are of many colours, shapes, sizes and materials, natural and man-made (there is a large body of antique button collectors). Buttonholes must be big enough to accommodate the button, may be eyed or straight, sewn with or without gimp, or piped, and may have separate bartacks to close the end for a cleaner, more expensive finish on tailored garments. Buttonholes are usually vertical on shirts and blouses and eyed and horizontal on jackets. Buttons are used functionally at any opening on the garment and decoratively anywhere, such as show buttons on double breasted jackets, and even comprehensively with pearly kings and queens.

Hooks and bars have their commonest use to fasten the top of a trouser fly. Both the hook and bar carry prongs which pass through the cloth and interlining and through holes in a metal backing plate where they are bent round to hold the backing plate firmly in position. The plate is covered by a backing fabric to prevent wear from the bent prongs on the fabric of the garment. This method provides the strongest fastening. Hooks and eyes perform the same function in miniature at the top of dress zips, for instance.

Press studs, which suffered a decline in use after the introduction of the zip, are now used in a more sophisticated form as a convenience fastening in babywear. Similarly they are widely used on denim jeans, skirts and jackets, together with tack buttons and rivets to strengthen the corners of pockets. The thread holding conventional buttons would be overstressed and would rapidly abrade. With all metal fasteners, where two pieces of metal grip fabric plies, it is crucial that the fastener does not lie over the edge of one of those plies or it will not fasten properly (Fig. 6.8).

Hook and loop fastening (common brand name Velcro) consists of two woven polyamide tapes, one covered with very fine hooks and the other with very fine loops. When pressed together they grip securely.

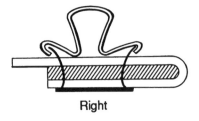

Right

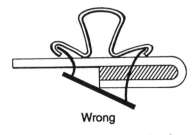

Wrong

Fig. 6.8 Metal fasteners: example of Duostud.

They cannot easily be pulled apart laterally, yet they peel apart easily. Both parts are sewn to the garment close to their edges, by two thread lockstitch. The limited range of use includes cuff and ankle openings on waterproof garments, where a person wearing gloves or mittens can operate the closure. Similarly this fastening is useful on garments worn by some disabled people.

Zip fasteners are used to close the flies of trousers, the openings of skirts and dresses, the fronts and pockets of anoraks, and on babywear and swimwear. The list could be be extended almost indefinitely. Zips have two edges, which mesh together and resist pulling apart when stressed, embedded in a tape support which is sewn into the garment. The tapes are usually woven of cotton, polyester, polyamides or mixtures. The meshing component can be individual teeth of brass, or more cheaply aluminium, and also plastic. A common alternative is a continuous spiral of plastic, usually polyamide. An end stop secures the zip at the bottom. The slider opens and closes the zip and locks the zip by means of a stop resting between the teeth. Sliders may be decorative or serve a special function, such as a ball and chain or large ring on skiwear, which gloved hands can grasp.

There are basically three finished appearances of the zip openings. Firstly, two folded edges can be brought together at the centre of the zip teeth and stitched in parallel rows to the tapes of the zip, leaving an opening in the middle down which the slider moves to open the zip. Secondly, one folded edge overlaps the other. The edge underneath is sewn close to the zip teeth but the edge on top is sewn somewhat away from the teeth to form a small fly. This method shows only one row of stitching on the surface. The third method is the so-called invisible zip, where the teeth are attached to the tape in a reverse manner, so that the slider works as it were through the back of the zip. The cloth is sewn to the zip tape very close to the teeth, with no stitching visible on the outside of the garment. This makes a zip opening which looks as much as possible like the extension of a sewn seam.

A further type is the zip which can be opened at the lower end in cardigans and jackets, which have to be completely open rather than stepped into. This type of zip may have magnified plastic teeth, which emphasise the sporting image of the garment, and may offer a contrasting colour or some other form of decorative interest. Finally zips with two sliders are needed on longer jackets, where the wearer might place undue strain on the jacket on sitting down. The lower slider can be pulled up, which opens the lower end of the zip.

Elastic, while not strictly a fastening, both allows access and grips the body after the garment has been put on. The simplest forms of assembly are waistband elastic at the top of trousers, shorts and pyjamas, and at the bottom of casual jackets. The wholly elastic girdle requires stitching with the same elastic properties as the fabric, such as a simple zig-zag or three-stitch zig-zag. When elastic is used to grip the waist in a self-supporting trouser, it is completely enclosed in a tunnel formed by the fabric of the trouser band and bandlining, with one end secured at the seat seam. The other end is covered with fabric and protrudes through a slot at the side waist. As the trouser is put on, the protruding end is drawn forward to be fastened by button and buttonholes, hook and bar or on a zip principle.

Pockets

Pockets are not an integral part of the construction of a garment, but are additions which allow the wearer to carry coins, wallet, notebook, keys, comb, golf tees, pens and so on. Traditionally women carry handbags and have fewer pockets, whereas men's garments demand pockets for every purpose, even up to the total of 14 commonly in a two piece suit. One property of a pocket is that it should not disturb the silhouette of a garment, while it adds decorative interest to the design. It must also be strong and of a size fit for its purpose.

Pockets may be divided into three broad classes according to the method of insertion: first the pocket which is simply sewn on to the surface of the garment, the patch principle; secondly the pocket which involves cutting through the surface of the fabric in order that the pocket bag may hang on the inside of the garment, the through principle; and thirdly the pocket which forms part of a seam, the inset principle. Pockets may also be analysed into the following parts

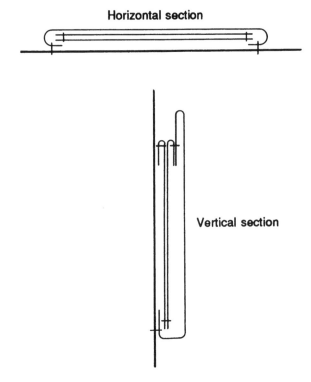

Horizontal section

Vertical section

Fig. 6.9 Bluffed on patch pocket.

essential to their function: the mouth, which allows the wearer's hand to enter the pocket; the bag; the facing, which is sewn on for aesthetic reasons to cover the joining of the pocket bag to the garment; and sometimes the flap to cover the pocket mouth.

Examples of the patch principle form a hierarchy. This begins with the simplest form of assembly, where the top edge is turned down, the edges are pressed under and the patch is stitched to the garment, as in a shirt. Here the top of the patch forms the pocket mouth and the patch itself forms the pocket bag. In a more sophisticated form, one ply of pocketing is sewn on to the patch, turned out, pressed and edge stitched on to the garment as above. This method avoids the presence of a raw edge of fabric inside the patch; and the ply of pocketing lends stability to the patch. Alternatively a complete pocket bag of two plies may be assembled, with the top edge sewn to the turned down patch at the front and to the garment at the back, the bag being loose inside the patch. With this method the patch is sewn from the inside to a previously marked line. This so-called bluffed on patch shows no stitching on the surface and is the most lengthy type of patch construction (Fig. 6.9).

The through principle demands a cut in the same line as the pocket

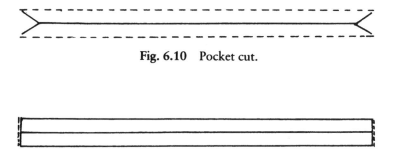

Fig. 6.10 Pocket cut.

Fig. 6.11 Pocket corners.

mouth; but in order to give width to the pocket mouth, the cut finishes at both ends with a V (Fig. 6.10). The underlying form of the pocket mouth is a long thin rectangle cut so that all four sides can fold back, the longer sides when jets which finish the mouth have been sewn on, the shorter Vs under the ends. The weakest points are the four corners of the rectangle. The effects of strain on the corners can be reduced by accurate tacking and backing the pocket mouth with a stay usually of fusible material. Either one or two jets fill in the rectangle of the mouth. The ends of the jets are passed under the ends of the pocket cut and the Vs are turned under and stitched on top of the jets (Fig. 6.11).

The inset principle starts from the idea that the pocket mouth is part of a seam. The edge of the pocket mouth follows the line of the seam and the closing of the seam completes the pocket mouth and closes the ends. Often the strain at the ends is taken by bartacks placed across the ends at right angles to the line of the seam. The inset principle is often used on an unlined garment. Hence, the pocket bag is closed with a French seam or safety stitch using a bulked thread (Fig. 6.12).

Surface decoration

The two largest groups of surface decoration are sewn decorations and pressed decorations.

The simplest form of sewn decoration is a line or lines of two thread lockstitch, closely parallel to a seam or an edge. The stitch type may be varied by 'saddle stitching' or the pick stitching (Type 209) which simulates hand stitching on the edges of jackets. Gathering draws up fabric by one or more threads to produce frills on edges or hems. Tucks are folds of fabric, holding fullness and used for shaping, appearing as pin tucks of very narrow width or graduated tucks on bodices, yokes and so on. Piping can be used on a seam or edge; it is made by covering cord of varying softness with fabric on the bias, or sometimes the lining fabric of a lined garment.

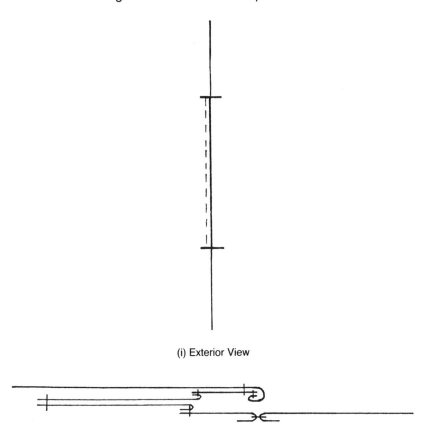

(i) Exterior View

(ii) Horizontal Cross-Section

Fig. 6.12 Inset pocket.

Three techniques are used to cover relatively large areas of the garment surface. Smocking is a way of stabilising fullness in even folds, often on the bodice. Shirring involves sewing with elastic thread to draw in waists and cuffs evenly and attractively. Quilting uses, commonly, two thread lockstitch, in square or diamond patterns, sewn through two plies of fabric with wadding between. Wadding or batting are the names given to fibre fillings which supply insulation without great weight. The commonest fibre is polyester of various diameters, solid or hollow. Many different weights and thicknesses of wadding can be produced by varying fibre, density of batt and thickness. With a fashion for widely spaced quilting, it is necessary to include a binding agent in the batt to prevent the wadding moving about or dropping. The designer of a quilted garment will choose that form of wadding and quilting construction which best meets the aesthetic and per-

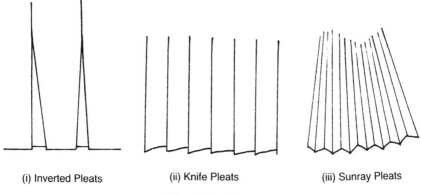

(i) Inverted Pleats   (ii) Knife Pleats   (iii) Sunray Pleats

Fig. 6.13 Pleats.

formance objectives of the garment: bulk, insulation and cost, and the shape and dimensions of the quilting. Finally when selecting fabric to enclose wadding it is important that its construction is close enough to prevent fibre ends working their way through the fabric to appear on the surface.

Pressing produces unsewn pleats or creases in many forms. The simplest is the crease in trouser legs. Pleating is a special type of pressing, which aims to produce an array of creases of some durability and according to a geometrical pattern. This may be an overall pattern of small pleats (crystal pleating or accordion pleating), formed by pleating a whole roll of cloth. Alternatively, in hand pleating, the fabric is folded between two complementary card patterns, which are scored in such a way as to fold at the lines where pleats are required. The resulting sandwich is then rolled up and put in a steam box or autoclave. This sets the pleats, whose durability is related to the temperature and duration of the steaming as well as to the nature of the fabric. Typical hand pleats are sunray pleats, knife pleats, box pleats and inverted pleats (Fig. 6.13).

Joining

One of the most important of the designer's decisions is the choice of stitch type to join or decorate the components of the garment referred to in most of the principles above. British Standard 3870: Part 1: 1982; Classification and Terminology of Stitch Types, is the standard reference for stitch types now available for use in garment construction. The British Standard describes 70 or so stitch types of which perhaps up to 20 are in regular use. Only high volume staple production regularly uses all of these; in small volume production perhaps only two or three types appear. A full analysis of these stitch

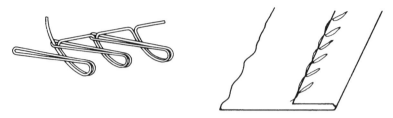

Fig. 6.14 Chainstitch blindstitch.

types can be found in Carr and Latham, *The Technology of Clothing Manufacture*, and Friend, *Sewing Room Technical Handbook*, HATRA (1977).

The sort of problem the designer might face is the choice of stitch for blindstitching the hem. The chainstitch version, type 103 (Fig. 6.14), uses a curved needle in order to penetrate only partially into the outer fabric before picking up the hem edge, thus showing minimally or not at all on the right side of the garment. In spite of a device which condenses stitches at the finishing end, the stitch tends to be insecure unless the thread end of the final stitch is through the correct loop. The incidence of customers' complaints about hems falling down is relatively high. The alternative is to use the lockstitch version, type 306 (Fig. 6.15). This is more secure than the traditional chainstitch blindstitch, but the stitch formation shows a straight bobbin thread which if snagged can allow sections of the stitching to come undone. On finer fabrics it may tend to pucker. An additional disadvantage is that it is much more difficult to remove without damaging the garment, if the customer wishes to alter the hem.

Five properties of seams relate to the discussion of stitch and seam type: strength, elasticity, durability, security and comfort.

Seam strength relates to the various modes of seam breakdown. It is relatively rare for stitching to break. The cause is usually a break in the seam which the operator has joined ineffectively. It is also rare for the fabric to rupture. The most common defect is when the seam opens up owing to what is usually known as seam slippage. This occurs in fabrics woven from slippery yarns, relatively loosely woven. The yarns parallel to the seam slide over those at right angles to the seam, when the seam is stressed transversely. It produces an unacceptable appearance, otherwise known as seam slippage, long before the seam actually breaks. Increasing the seam allowance and changing the seam type to, say, a lap felled seam may help. In practice, many fabrics are unsuitable for making up into close-fitting garment styles. Fabrics should be investigated at the design stage by means of the standard tests for seam slippage and by wearer trials.

The above applies to woven fabrics. Knitted fabrics are normally

Fig. 6.15 Lockstitch blindstitch.

more extensible. A stitch type must be selected with an extensibility greater than that of the fabric. In other words, in knitted fabrics the behaviour of seams under longitudinal stress is of much greater importance than the behaviour under transverse stress.

The seam elasticity required in stretch fabrics (up to 100%) cannot be achieved using two thread lockstitch or two thread chainstitch. The designer has to choose from overedge stitch, lockstitch zig-zag and class 600 covering stitches, although the seam types are then limited. Lower amounts of stretch can be coped with by lockstitch or chainstitch, using an accurately balanced stitch, perhaps a higher stitch density and synthetic threads.

Seam durability relates mainly to the amount of abrasion suffered by the stitched thread lying on the surface of the garment. The most important factor is how far the thread beds into the fabric. The exposed surface of a balanced lockstitch has much better resistance to abrasion than the exposed underside of a multi-thread chainstitch. Stitchings at high tension are much less susceptible to abrasion than those at low tensions. In addition, a needle thread to looper thread ratio of 1:1 allows the stitch loops to be spaced out and thus bed in better. Seams sewn in a densely woven or coated fabric cannot easily bed in and are therefore more quickly abraded than those sewn in softer fabrics. A typical example is the abrasion on the inside leg of denim jeans. The traditional jeans seam consists of a lap felled seam with two rows of two thread chainstitch. The stitches abrade rapidly especially when the jeans are tight on the leg of a heavily built wearer. Many manufacturers adopt the solution of superimposed seams sewn with safety stitch.

A special case is the buttonhole. Synthetic threads give better performance than cotton; and spun polyester or corespun (a cotton core covered with cotton or polyester) thread give longer life and good appearance. Silk thread (especially undegummed) gives excellent service in buttonholes, but is more expensive. One source of abrasion is the shank of the button lying in the buttonhole; continuous filament button thread may seriously shorten the life of the buttonhole by abrading the spun fibre thread.

Seam security, in addition to all the points made above, relates also to the type of stitch used. The most secure type is normally the lockstitch. The least secure is usually the single thread chainstitch (Class 100). Here, each loop of thread secures the preceding loop. This simple arrangement of thread applies very little friction, especially in the blind felling version discussed above. If the last stitch is not correctly locked, if a thread is snagged, or if a stitch slips during sewing, it will run very easily. Much blind felling, buttonsewing, buttonholing and multi-needle stitching in bulk garment production uses this stitch. Considerable customer dissatisfaction following seam failure has not eliminated these stitches because the machines which produce them are fast, usually of lower price than their lockstitch equivalents, and would entail a large reinvestment to replace. Stitch condensation, referred to earlier in discussion of type 103, and proper selection of threads can inhibit the tendency to run.

Multi-thread chainstitch, overedging stitches and covering chain stitches (Classes 400, 500, 600) are generally reckoned to show a security level somewhere between lockstitch and single thread chain-stitch. Their looping arrangements are much more complex. Al-though running is still possible it is inhibited by the increased friction among the loops and the probable tangling of the thread in the loops before it has run very far. The simplest, 401 two thread chainstitch, is the most likely to run. An important consideration in designing the construction of the garment is to ensure that weak ends of seams are protected by sewing across. When all else fails it may be necessary to bar-tack the end of the chain separately.

Comfort is difficult to measure but there are several known causes of discomfort such as bulky seam types and monofilament polyamide threads, especially if the garment is too small for the wearer. This is quite apart from label discomfort, mentioned earlier.

Apart from various forms of damage to the seam and malformations of stitches, the commonest problem which gives both designers and customers dissatisfaction is seam pucker. Pucker is a wrinkling or fullness or slight bubbling along the line of the seam. This reduces customer appeal by disturbing the smooth finish of the garment. Possible causes include fabric structure, seam construction, needle size, feeding problems, incorrect thread tensions and unsuitable thread. Pucker may appear immediately or only after pressing or washing. There are many fabrics of loose weave with soft yarns, which rarely show pucker. In contrast many smooth, fine, synthetic fabrics are almost impossible to sew without some pucker. Machinists who work on these fabrics, where some pucker has to be accepted, find it difficult to achieve the minimum possible at all times. Attempts have been made to define standards of pucker through photographs and sewn examples, but these are not always satisfactory. Hence it is the subjective judgement of inspectors, quality controllers and ultimately the designer that maintains the standards.

Testing fabrics for 'sewability' should be an important influence on their choice. Too often fabrics are selected because of their aesthetic qualities without considering their performance in making up. Two methods have been available for some time. The Hatra Sew is used with a sewing machine and measures the temperature reached by the sewing needle while sewing the test fabric, using an infra-red detection device. The L & M Sewability Tester works without a sewing machine, measuring the force required to push a needle through a fabric.

Finishing

Pressing makes a large contribution to the finished appearance of garments and thus their attractiveness at the point of sale. The objectives of pressing are:

(1)   To smooth away unwanted creases and crush marks.
(2)   To make creases where the design of the garment requires them. Creases are used not only on trouser legs and as an array in pleating, but front edges and sewn seams are in effect creases joined together.
(3)   To mould the garment to the contour of the body, especially in tailored garments (referred to in the section on pattern cutting in Chapter 2). The chief areas where this takes place are around the ends of darts, collars, shoulders, armholes and sleeveheads, and sometimes trouser legs. A general principle can be stated: where the body has a prominence extra length is created, and where the body has a hollow the fabric is shrunk.
(4)   To refinish the fabric after manufacturing the garment. The presser must remove glazing and lift up nap or pile flattened during underpressing–in short return the fabric to the richness intended by the designer.
(5)   During the manufacturing process underpressing prepares the garment for further sewing, makes it easier and makes better quality sewing possible.

Garments fall into five categories in relation to pressing:

(1)   Garments which require no pressing include foundationwear, stretch swimwear and dancewear, briefs and other items of underwear.
(2)   Garments which require minimal finishing are steamed and dried, using various equipment, simply to relax the crushes and light creases which may be present. These garments are of two types:

single ply garments such as slips and nightgowns, often in knitted synthetics, and quilted or wadded garments such as anoraks.

(3) Garments requiring ironing in underpressing and final pressing use simple but flexible equipment for an output with continuous style change, very often with small areas of interlining and unlined. It would be uneconomic to install steam pressing with individually shaped bucks, because the quantity per style is too small.

(4) Extensive underpressing and final pressing require the pressing open of seams and the setting of edges during manufacture. Large areas are moulded, there are large areas of interlining and the garments are usually lined. This group includes men's jackets, trousers and waistcoats, many skirts, women's tailored jackets and trousers, topcoats, trench coats and other lined rainwear. Radical style change in many of these garments is infrequent and a range of specialised, shaped presses has been developed, because the investment in them can be recovered over a relatively large quantity of garments.

One example is trouser pressing, conventionally carried out in two operations: legging on a flat press which sets and creases the legs, and topping in a series of lays around the top on a contoured press. If the trouser features a pleat, the leg crease has to be run into it accurately, probably in a separate lay. The problem is to provide firmly set creases at the same time as an even finish to the fabric overall, without impressions of pockets, fly and seams showing. Traditionally, these impressions were removed in a subsequent 'touching up' operation with an iron on those fabrics such as gaberdines where the steam press leaves an unacceptable finish, but on most fabrics this should not be necessary. Trouser legging also moulds the leg by pressing away fullness in the underside below the seat area, and by shaping the calves in closer fitting trousers. In addition the presser must set the crease in the correct position in order that it might hang centrally over the shoe of the wearer. Usually the pattern cutter designs the pattern in such a way that the presser achieves the desired effect by aligning the inside leg seam with the outside leg seam to the knee, and the inside leg seam then runs back a few centimetres at the crotch.

(5) The 'permanent press' process was developed some years ago as a way of providing good crease recovery after washing to cellulosic fabrics. It declined with the rise in popularity of polyester blends, where the polyester content assists crease recovery and improves fabric strength, while permanent press treatment reduces fabric strength.

More recently, in an attempt to compete with man-made fibres, the process has been marketed again with 100 per cent cotton fabrics of high enough initial strength to allow for some degradation. The process involves treating fabric during manufacture with a post-curing resin (in constrast to pre-cured, resinated, crease resistant fabric which would be cured at high temperature before delivery). The post-cure process is often used for trousers. Here the creases are formed and the garment pressed, and the trousers are then passed through an oven in order to cure the fabric at high temperature. When the garment is washed and dried it returns to the shape as cured, smooth across the panels and creased where required. It is the responsibility of the designer to select fabrics and trims which resist the high temperatures of the curing oven, particular problems being dye migration and shrinkage.

Fabric classification

What is largely missing from the preceding principles is an analysis of the design implications of the fabric being joined and finished, and its influence on construction methods. From the origins of the research programme in the 1970s, Sueo Kawabata at Kyoto University and Richard Postle at the University of New South Wales have, with their teams of associates, developed and published, especially in the 1980s, many papers and several symposia centring on 'The Kawabata System for the Standardisation and Analysis of Hand Evaluation'.

The programme, using expert panels, selected the terms to be used to describe fabric handle (such as stiffness, smoothness, fullness and softness, crispness, and so on). It defined the terms and developed rating scales for them. A large number of fabrics were rated by many skilled individuals. The programme then isolated six groups of mechanical properties of fabric: tensile, bending, shearing, compression, surface, weight and thickness. Each of these properties has several related factors, which result in 16 values. Kawabata developed four precision instruments to measure these mechanical properties and allow the calculation of the 16 values. The correlation between the ratings of fabric handle by the expert panels and the measurement of mechanical properties was very high.

The significant point is that, whereas the first results of this programme related to design characteristics of fabrics, it was envisaged from the beginning that the mechanical properties would also relate to manufacturing parameters such as sewability and tailorability. Profiles have been developed that define which range for the 16 values indicates a fabric which is easy to manufacture; outside that range, appropriate extra work and more control of the process are needed. The mechanical properties can also be related to specific problems. For example, fabrics which are prone to seam pucker are classified under 'tensile' as being less extensible and less elastic in extension, under 'bending' inelastic, and light in weight. Further extensions of the programme are predicting the effect of fabric finishing methods, weave structure, yarn type and fibre on both handle and behaviour during manufacture. There are a number of instances of new fabric developments designed to exhibit specific mechanical properties and achieve target fabric properties of handle and behaviour.

This account is of course very short and cannot possibly do justice to all the facets of the system which Kawabata has placed in the hands of both fabric designers and clothing designers.

Conclusion

Since the 1940s predetermined motion time systems (PMTS) have been developed which allow estimation of work content at a very early stage in the design process. The most well used of these is Methods Time Measurement (MTM). The first system used very tiny elements of time and is now mainly a research tool. Subsequently, systems employing larger elements were developed, some for specific industrial applications. In the clothing field one of the best known is Garment Sewing Data (GSD). This system is computerised and enables rapid estimation of work content, and hence direct labour cost, at the sample stage.

Using some of the ideas of group technology it should be possible to extend this concept further, especially with the availability of computers. Group technology depends on effective coding and classification methods. It enables similar items to be classified together and thus facilitates control of variety during design. In its full form it is concerned with processing components or features in combined batches in order to obtain the benefits of longer runs. A basic product element is defined as part of a product which has its own purpose and which is used in its entirety in the formation of another product. A basic element must have its own purpose, and must be interchangeable with another basic element having the same function.

Basic elements of a clothing classification might be seams, collars, cuffs, sleeve openings, pockets, hems and so on. The objectives of classifying are to provide a library of information about new designs, to retrieve a pattern which may need only slight modification, to retrieve a method of construction, to know the direct costs of both material and labour and to retrieve the design of workplaces and manufacturing sequence. The classification could never be totally comprehensive because a fashion industry is always likely to throw up new items, but coverage of the great majority would be achieved over time. It would enable a comparison to be made of available variations for features in the design, in relation to the requirements of the manufacturing method and the costs; all the ways of constructing a sleeve opening could be studied, and a design decision made bearing in mind all the facts. If information is not rapidly available it tends not to be sought, perhaps until after a decision has been made intuitively. Design not only uses imagination but selects from information. Classification of construction methods according to design purpose may not only assist the effectiveness of design but also eventually provide the architecture to link the islands of automation in a fully computer integrated manufacture.

7

Costs and Profits

There is nothing so certain in running a clothing business as the fact that sales revenue minus costs equals profit. A business must plan to achieve a level of sales revenue, to incur a level of costs and thus generate a level of profit. These planned levels do not necessarily coincide with actual revenues, costs and profits. Hence managers spend a large part of their time controlling the activities of a business in order to maintain the planned level of profit. This chapter explores the interaction of financial planning and control with the processes of fashion design and product development.

Sales revenue

The sales revenue from a style of garment is the price per garment multiplied by the volume sold. This may vary from a unique garment sold to an individual customer to tens of thousands of garments sold through retail outlets. The unique garment attracts a very high price because the customer perceives the value of what the garment does for him or her as very high, and because uniqueness implies less price competition. Of course the costs also are very high, because they absorb in one garment all the costs of design and development, and because in making the garment there are fewer opportunities to make those savings which come from repetition. On the other hand large quantities of the same garment style attract a lower price because the customer perceives the value of what may have the status of a 'commodity' garment as much lower, and the large quantities imply a large market with substantial price competition. Of course the costs also are lower, because there are many garments to share the costs of design and development, and because in making large quantities many opportunities occur to save time and cost from repetition and the engineering of production.

Price

When discussing price in a competitive market it is important to distinguish the retail price from the manufacturer's price; the difference between the two is usually referred to as mark-up. All three are variable as they interact with each other and with customer perceptions.

Although the manufacturer's price and the cost of garments influence each other, the planned price is, with few exceptions, determined independently of the planned cost. One pricing objective seeks a satisfactory profit in the interest of a continuing profit in the future, even though a higher price might produce a larger immediate profit. Another pricing objective is market penetration, when the price is low enough to discourage competition, when the market is price sensitive and when the cost per garment decreases with increased volume. Again the company may propose a price which aims to 'skim' the market.

Customers will pay a higher price for benefits such as quick delivery, fashion innovation, exclusivity and the supplying of very small orders, because these factors have a high value for the customer. This occurs when a number of buyers seek to buy and the price is relatively inelastic, when the type of garment is such that the increased cost of manufacturing fewer garments is covered by charging what the market will bear, and when there is little danger that the higher price will stimulate the emergence of more sources of supply to provide competition. Sometimes a higher price will itself induce a perception of higher value by the customer. There are many examples of an increase in price stimulating an increase in sales. Sometimes a manufacturer may seek a price which will guarantee early recovery of his investment in specialised machinery, which he may have bought for an established customer's special request, and when he is unsure about the level of its future use. Finally, the manufacturer (or retailer) may attempt to promote a range of styles and maximise profit over the entire range by offering a 'loss leader' at an artificially low price.

In addition to all the pricing strategies they may adopt, the manufacturers and retailers will allow for a percentage of markdowns – garments sold at the end of a range, when their time is past. Good planning of course keeps this percentage as low as possible.

Whatever the strategy employed, a number of factors determine price. One is the customer's perception of the style or fashion content, the innovation or uniqueness of the style, the value of the fabric and trims (cashmere versus acrylic, silk versus polyester/cotton), and the value of the work content (hand stitched edges on men's suit jackets, lining in skirts). The level of competition from other manufacturers in the buying offices of the customer may be the most important influence. Again if a manufacturer supplies wholly or mainly one customer it is too simple to say that the buying power of the customer drives the manufacturer's prices down, for manufacturer and customer have a two-way relationship. This leads to a deeper exploration of cost structures by the buyer to obtain both a reasonable price and a reasonable profit to the manufacturer, to ensure he continues in business and continues to invest. Hence the size and length of contracts is another influence on price.

Volume

The other component of sales revenue is volume. Volume and price react on each other in both the long and the short term. Volume in one sense is the number of outlets multiplied by the sales in each. Total sales volume comes from the length of time the style is sustained in the market. A staple or commodity garment, relatively free from the imperatives of fashion, may go on selling from season to season, its volume affected perhaps by longer term economic influences. A fashion garment may sell a very large volume over a very short period, when for instance a favourite character in a soap opera wears it in a television programme or when a member of the royal family wears it at her marriage.

Manufacturers make predictions of the sales volumes of individual styles often only after they have sold some of their season's garments, projecting from the sample estimates of the whole output. Both retailers and manufacturers will predict sales volume from the actual sales of similar styles achieved in previous seasons, as well as what is happening to colour, shape and design detail in markets which they deem to be 'ahead' of their market – in other countries or on the catwalks of well known designers.

Manufacturing costs

Costs of manufacturing businesses are divided by cost accountants broadly into material costs, labour costs and overheads. Manufacturing overheads may be separated from other overheads in order that the total cost of manufacturing alone may be known and controlled. In addition a further category, of direct manufacturing expenses, may have to be included: namely such items as pleating and embroidery – services purchased in the same way as materials. Thus it becomes clear that varying language, planning and control forms and categories will give rise to different methods of reporting costs in each company.

Material costs

Budget (or planned) direct material costs comprise two components: the standard price per metre multiplied by standard usage. Standard usage in the clothing industry is called the material estimate. The standard price per metre is based on the current price plus estimates of increases and estimates of reductions for larger quantities. (The word standard here implies a standard against which actual usage will be judged and is a prediction or estimate of what will happen.)

The design and development process affects the price per metre simply by choosing one fabric or trim instead of another, but it also affects the material estimate in a number of ways. The material estimate is not a simple figure, but is made up of a number of components. In theory it can be viewed as a series of averages plus a series of allowances for losses. A full analysis would identify three sorts of averaging:

(1) a weighted average marker length over a series of sizes, based on predictions about the proportions of sales in the various sizes;
(2) averaging of marker lengths for expected fabric widths;
(3) averaging over a number of predicted marker combinations (single garment markers, two garment markers, four garment markers and so on).

Clearly larger sizes take more cloth and smaller sizes consume less. The precise amount of increase or decrease per size cannot be predicted but useful averages based on past experience with similar sets of shapes can be extrapolated. Again wider markers mean shorter markers, usually consuming less fabric; and wider fabric is often proportionately less expensive. Further, generally speaking, the more garments there are in a marker the smaller the amount of fabric per garment because there are more opportunities to fit pattern edges closer together. The material estimate also includes allowances for unavoidable fabric losses: end losses over and above the marker length of each ply in a spread, fabric lost in cutting out flaws and damages, and unusable fabric remnants at the end of pieces. Universally, clothing manufacturers attempt to minimise their material estimates, especially because direct material cost represents on average 50 per cent of total cost.

At one extreme manufacturers of staple garments, making large quantities of one style, will spend much more time on research into their material estimates. Accuracy about costs is more important in the face of keen price competition. With a longer planning cycle they also have the time. At the other extreme manufacturers of fashion garments are more likely to take the line of for instance 'size 14 plus 10 per cent', because they do not have the time to do more, and because competition centres on fashion innovation rather than just price competition.

In research carried out as long ago as 1970, B. Trautman in *Material Utilisation in the Apparel Industry* found that, averaging over a number of garment types, approximately 90 per cent of fabric went into the garment. The other 10 per cent was lost in the ways listed above, the biggest loss being in the marker. Of the 90 per cent just over half was required simply to cover the human body in the area of the garment. The other half provided ease, drape, style, fashion and seams, turnings, inlays and turnups. This is by no means to suggest that designers should make substantial savings in this area, because it is precisely in this use of 45 per cent of the fabric that designers create garments that customers wish to buy. Only in an age of austerity with utility clothing were restrictions placed on what designers might do with fabric.

Marker planning

Design and development have most effect on the material estimate in the planning of markers. Marker making can be viewed in two ways: as the first operation in the manufacturing process or as an operation in the design and development process. This is the first operation in which all the pattern pieces are studied together inside the rectangle of a marker, as well as in relation to the fabric from which the garment parts will be cut.

The marker maker must be prepared to feed information about the material estimate into the design and product development process, in order that decisions about the commercial profitability of a style may be taken. This may be used at the initial range meetings as well as later, during commercial development.

Apart from inherent technical requirements, such as good definition of line, accuracy of reproduction of the pattern, correct pattern count and correct labelling of pattern parts, the technical requirements of a marker relate to the characteristics of the fabric:

(1) *Pattern alignment* in relation to the grain of the fabric. Pattern pieces normally carry a grain line which signifies where the vertical is when the garment is worn. With most large patterns, the grain line should lie parallel to the warp of a woven fabric or the wales of a knitted fabric. Often the designer or pattern cutter defines a tolerance which allows the marker maker to swing the grain line a small amount from parallel. If the marker maker swings a pattern too much, the finished garment will not hang and drape correctly when worn. Of course this restricts the freedom the marker maker has in choosing how to lay patterns in the marker. The decision about the amount of tolerance allowed

is an empirical decision, balancing the fabric saving arising from the tighter placing of patterns against the effect in the finished garment. The properties of the fabric and the price level of the garment in the chosen market segment influence this decision.

(2) *Pattern facing*. Asymmetrical or one way fabrics are of two types. One way only fabrics are those with a heavy surface pile or nap, such as velvet, and those with a recognisable pattern such as plants or animals. The top end of all pieces in the finished garment should point in the same direction, for an acceptable aesthetic effect. One way either way fabrics include one way checks and stripes, where the sequence of colours is only half repeated, and many knitted fabrics, where the structure of the loops reflects light differently in different directions. This means again that all the pattern pieces should point in the same direction, but either direction is acceptable in the finished garment. Laying the patterns indiscriminately would produce unacceptable mirror images in vertical stripes, unmatchable checks and the appearance of shading in many knitted fabrics.

Almost always the restrictions of a one way fabric produce a longer marker than in a symmetrical fabric. In the case of one way only fabrics this result has to be accepted, with a consequent increase in material cost. On the other hand the push of cost against price can be tolerated because of the higher perceived value in what are usually specialist garments. In the case of one way either way fabrics there are two courses open to the manufacturer. The marker maker may lay two garments (or more) in the marker, one complete set of patterns in each direction, which achieves a tighter placement. Or the designer may scrutinise the make-up of a one way check or stripe; in some cases, in the more complex designs of fabric, the aesthetic effect may be maintained, or almost maintained, were the fabric to be symmetrical. This is not of course to deny the unique effects obtainable from many one way fabric designs. Nor does it answer immediate problems of fabric usage. It implies a continuous pressure on fabric suppliers to reconsider one way designs where appropriate.

(3) *Vertical stripes*. Here there is little possibility of any tolerance from grain lines. Again, parts such as pockets and flaps may have to be matched, which restricts their position in the marker. The marker maker may have to place facings for lapels and fronts of jackets in such a way that the prominent stripe is not close to the finished edges. Further, in an effect most clearly seen on high contrast candy stripes, it is necessary to avoid the clash of either light or dark stripes in part of a finished seam (Fig. 7.1). Finally, if the vertical stripes of a collar are to match the back of a garment

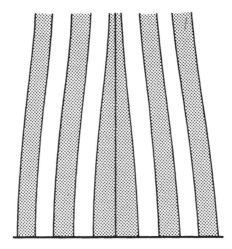

Fig. 7.1 Clash of stripes.

with a centre back seam, then not only must the collar be centralised but the back must be cut so that after seaming it matches the collar. All these adjustments mean more space between patterns and a longer marker.

(4) *Checks*. All the above remarks concerning vertical stripes apply to checks; but checks use even more fabric because in many places they have to match both vertically and horizontally. The customer and the designer define the matching points on a garment, either by tradition or specification. These points generally include main body seams, sleeve seams, sleeve to body, collars, pockets and waistband sections. Usually the higher the selling price and the more prominent the check, the greater the number of matching points and the greater the restriction on the positioning of patterns in the marker. One of the most extreme examples is tartan fabrics where the checks are not only large but use high contrast, primary colours. Here seams not normally matched, such as forearm seams on jackets, may require matching. The positioning of checks in relation to garment edges and seams and the centre front of skirts demands considerable movement of patterns within the marker, both vertically and horizontally.

Given the achievement of technical objectives, which relate to the quality of finished garments, marker making aims to economise on the use of fabrics by planning the placement of pattern pieces to make the shortest marker. The clothing manufacturer has always paid great attention to the planning of markers, because when the cutting room cuts cloth it effectively spends half the manufacturing cost. Any reduction in the amount of cloth used leads directly to increased profit.

Marker planning is a conceptual, intuitive, open and creative process, in contrast to making up a jigsaw puzzle, which is an analytical, step-by-step and closed process. There is no final solution to a marker making problem, only a tighter and therefore shorter marker the more time is spent on it. Since most of the pieces are irregular and often taper, one skill lies in discovering those edges which fit together most nearly, and placing side by side across the marker those patterns which fit the width most nearly. The planner will try a number of pattern placements, selecting the one which gives the shortest marker. The planner measures success in marker efficiency. A formula describes this:

$$\text{Marker efficiency} = \frac{\text{Area of patterns of the marker}}{\text{Total area of the marker}} \times 100$$

Since the reduction in material cost is so important, the planner has to discover opportunities for improvement in marker efficiency by altering the patterns and the fabric, the two elements brought together in marker planning.

Pattern engineering

The first opportunities are commonly designated pattern engineering.

First, the planner may spot opportunities arising from needlessly generous seams, turnings, hems and alteration allowances. In addition it is sometimes possible to cut 3–4 mm from the prominent corners of

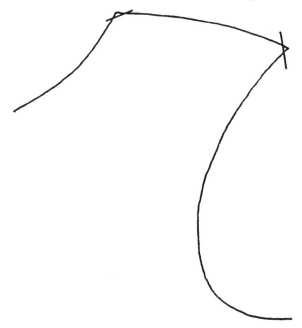

Fig. 7.2 Seam allowances.

Fig. 7.3 Piecing a facing.

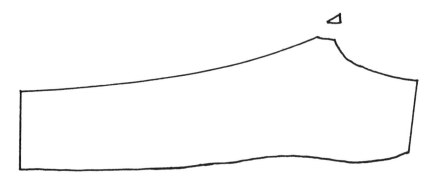

Fig. 7.4 Piecing a fork.

seam allowances (Fig. 7.2), to enable tighter placement of patterns, as long as this does not impair the security of finished garments.

Secondly, there may be an opportunity to 'piece' a pattern. This means dividing a large, awkwardly shaped pattern into two pieces, a large and a small, to accommodate it better in the marker. One example is the facing on a coat or jacket (Fig. 7.3). While this may save several centimetres on the length of the marker – a saving which has to be more than the extra labour cost of seaming it back together – the properties of the fabric often inhibit 'piecing'. This method introduces a horizontal seam into the front edge; solid weave or bulk may produce an unavoidable bump in the line of the front edge. In addition, the presence of a seam in the facing may be unacceptable in higher priced garments.

Another example is to piece the fork on the back or underside of trousers (Fig. 7.4). Here the prominence of the underside makes for considerable difficulty in the tight placement of this pattern in the marker. To separate 2–4 cm may enable as much as 10 cm per garment to be saved in a two-piece suit marker. The labour cost of overlocking, sewing and pressing the seam is usually considerably less than the cost saving in fabric. Once again a bulky fabric will prevent this method being used. The relationship with price is not simple. For many years, in the cut-make-and-trim business, when an individual larger customer presented a length of fabric which was short for making up into a suit, the cutter would piece the fork in order to fit the patterns into the length provided. Again the willingness to use this technique appears stronger in the industries of some EC countries than in the UK.

In both these examples the commercial attitude balances the cost saving against the effect on the finished garment and arrives at a decision in the light of all the factors.

Thirdly, the planner examines the location of seams to ensure the best placement of patterns, particularly of large panels lying side by side across the whole width of the fabric. Trial and error will suggest the best number of garments to include in the marker to be able to square off the end. When the large parts are laid out it may appear that, however the patterns are rearranged, some of the patterns across the piece are slightly too wide and some slightly too narrow. The transfer of material from the wide sections to the narrow sections might allow both to fit the total width of the marker, making better use of the marker than leaving a large empty space (Fig. 7.5).

The transfer results in the position of the seam being shifted in the finished garment. Often 1 cm is enough. It goes without saying that the seam shift should not affect the appearance or balance of the garment in such a way that the designer's intentions are significantly diverted. If no change is made, at least the effect of not making the change can be analysed, and the costs of the two alternatives will be known.

Fabric width

The second type of opportunity for improving marker efficiency arises in the influence the marker planner has on the selection of fabric width.

Fronts Backs

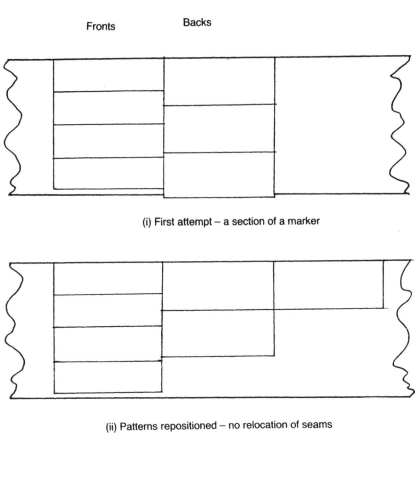

(i) First attempt – a section of a marker

(ii) Patterns repositioned – no relocation of seams

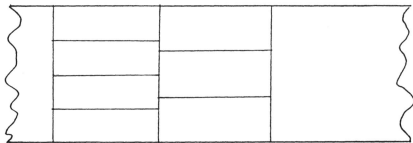

(iii) Relocation of seams in order to fit
panels into width of marker

Fig. 7.5 Seam location.

Within technical constraints the 'best' width depends, among other factors, on the costs of the various fabric widths per square metre, the typical number of garments in a marker, potential pattern engineering changes for various widths and the marker efficiency of a series of test markers.

Seasonality

In a staple manufacturing business making styles which carry over from one season to another, there is usually an opportunity to use up all the fabric purchased, perhaps with a very small markdown. On the other hand, in a fashion business this opportunity may occur less readily. For instance, a company orders 10 000 metres of fabric for a style as follows:

4 000	Red
2 000	Yellow
2 000	Blue
2 000	Green
10 000	

Sales of garments consume:

3500	Red
2000	Yellow
1800	Blue
1200	Green
8500	

This leaves 1500 metres unused which is sold off at £1 per metre, considerably less than the £5 per metre originally paid.

Hence the true cost is not £5 per metre but

$$\frac{(£5 \times 10\,000\,\text{m}) - £1\,500}{8\,500} = £5.71 \text{ per metre}$$

In fashion oriented companies precise prediction of sales and hence fabric usage is often more important than the fine tuning of fabric utilisation in the cutting room.

Labour costs

Direct labour cost includes cutters, sewers and pressers. Sewers and pressers typically comprise 95 per cent of the total. Direct labour cost normally varies from 20 to 25 per cent of total cost. There are some notable exceptions: the labour cost of manufacturing bras varies

Table 7.1 Weekly sewing room labour cost.

	Budget
(1) Standard hours output	3 840
(2) Overall performance per operator	80
(3) Attendance hours $\left\{3840 \times \dfrac{100}{80}\right\}$	4 800
(4) Pay rate per hour	£3.00
(5) Total wages paid (4800 × £3.00)	£14 400
(6) Cost per standard hour $\left\{\dfrac{14\,400}{3\,840}\right\}$	£3.75

Table 7.2 Example of output per week.

Style	Quantity	Standard time	Standard minutes output
A	5500	30	= 165 000
B	3000	20	= 60 000
C	360	15	= 5 400
Total			= 230 400
			= 3 840 standard hours

around 33 per cent of total cost and of overcoats around 60 per cent because of the amounts of fabric in relation to amounts of sewing.

In cost accounting terms the standard (or predicted) labour cost is:

standard price of labour × standard time.

In a staple garment company it is readily possible to predict the factors which influence these two components. For instance, the weekly sewing room labour cost might be stated as in Table 7.1.

The preparation of such a labour cost control statement begins with an agreement between marketing and production about a sales/production plan for the season. For marketing this is the volume of sales in each type and style of garment. For production this divides into an output per week, expressed in the common denominator of standard hours. An example of one week is shown in Table 7.2.

Production managers then predict what overall performance against standard (100) the operators in the sewing room will achieve. This is almost always less than standard because labour turnover means some operators are not yet fully skilled, and operators from time to time are engaged in activities other than sewing garments, sometimes called 'off standard' (waiting for machine repairs, extra unmeasured work or alterations).

Table 7.3 Example of direct labour cost.

Style	Standard time	Direct labour cost
A	30 min	£1.875
B	20 min	£1.25
C	15 min	£0.938

Given a requirement for an output of 3840 standard hours per week and a predicted overall performance of 80, the attendance hours (worked hours) required to produce this output are:

$$3840 \times \frac{100}{80} = 4800 \text{ attendance hours}$$

This could comprise simply 120 operators working for 40 hours each, but with a given rate of absence and part time employment it will in fact mean employing more than 120 on the payroll.

The pay rate per hour – the average gross wages operators will achieve – is based on competition in the local labour market to recruit and retain employees, government legislation about minimum wages and agreements with trade unions. In simple terms it originates from the company's pay rate last season plus predicted increases.

The total wages paid are the average pay rate per hour multiplied by the total attendance hours.

The cost per standard hour is the total wages paid divided by the output of standard hours:

$$\frac{£14\,400}{3\,840} = £3.75 \text{ per standard hour}$$

The result for our example is shown in Table 7.3.

This approach to labour cost is called process costing. Here successive orders of garments are not separated for costing purposes, but are accumulated over a week and the cost per standard hour is calculated as an average. Hence the exact labour cost of each order is impossible to determine. This approach assumes a relatively sophisticated management employing work study engineers, cost accountants and production planners, who design well balanced production lines, produce regular cost control information and ensure a continuous flow of garments.

In a fashion company with many styles, frequent changes and varying sizes of order, it is possible to estimate standard times but the prediction of actual working time is much more difficult because operators' learning time on a new style is both variable and significant. The overall performance is likely to be lower. More importantly, the learning time on short runs may never actually progress very far. Here one approach is to record the actual time taken on day one and then on successive days as the time taken reduces. A more complex approach might be to analyse the operations on new styles in terms of a number of factors such as fabric difficulty, length of operation, amount of operation that is new and so on, in order to estimate a pay premium in addition to the rate per standard hour, which would diminish over time.

Another method applies in subcontracting manufacturing companies. Having obtained a manufacturing price, the subcontractor takes away his fixed overheads and profit to leave the labour cost, which is divided as wages among his workers. Alternatively, to maintain wages at a level sufficient to retain his workers, the subcontractor will reduce his profit.

Whatever the time or cost arrived at, this information must be fed into the decision making process just like the information about material costs.

The design and product development process affects first the standard time, which measures the work content of the garment style. The designer presents a design which shows the separate features, to estimate the work content. This is where adaptation, compromise and discussion begin in an attempt to reach a standard time and hence a labour cost which will yield an agreed profit at the price expected for the garment style.

For instance, a bluffed on patch pocket with a separate pocket bag inside may produce the most acceptable result, but a single patch top stitched from the outside is simpler and quicker. Similarly a seam with two edges overlocked separately, chainstitched and pressed open produces the flattest, cleanest result on trouser legs, but safety stitching, comprising a simultaneous line of chainstitch and overlocking of the two edges together with subsequent pressing of the seam edges to one side, is simpler and quicker.

Again, on many garments the armhole and sleeve are completely constructed before the sleeve is inserted into the armhole. On others the underarm seam and the side seam are left open, the sleeve is sewn into the armhole while it is still flat, and finally the side seam and the underarm seam are closed in one line of stitching. This is simpler and quicker but the top of the underarm seam and the top of the side seam must marry in the garment design.

The design and product development process also affects the actual making time and hence the overall performance. The greater the number of styles in the range the more the operators will change their method of working, enter a new learning phase, and reduce their pace of working and thus their output. Not only will operators' pace be slower more often, but the amount of time operators are engaged on other activities will increase; more unmeasured work, more alterations and so on. Further, the creation of a range of very disparate styles requiring extreme changes of method from the operators will exacerbate this, but if the design process can create styles which appear new and different but in fact make use of a smaller range of skills and methods, then the loss of performance and output will be much less.

Overheads

Manufacturing overheads include payments such as: rent, local authority rates and insurance; the additional costs of employing people, such as sick pay, holiday pay and social costs; quality costs, comprising prevention, inspection and failure costs; maintenance and repair of buildings and machinery; salaries of managers and supervisors; clerical and storekeeping costs; industrial engineering; production planning and control; personnel, training and welfare expenses; costs of cleaning, security and safety; the cost of services such as power, steam, lighting and heating; and also depreciation, the cost of the use of owned assets.

Other overheads include: marketing, including sales office, representatives' salaries, commission and expenses, advertising including brochures, price lists and swatches; discounts; distribution overheads which include warehousing, packing, invoicing and delivery; and design and product development which comprise designers' salaries, expenses and equipment, the costs of pattern cutting and the costs of running and maintaining a sample room.

The design and product development process adds its own expenses to the total overhead cost, but also, through the range and complexity of the styles created, adds to training costs, industrial engineering costs and the expenses of planning and controlling production.

Total overhead expenses in a clothing manufacturing company usually vary from 25 to 30 per cent of total cost and are sometimes more.

In a fully developed system of cost accounting, overheads are dealt with in four stages:

(1) Payments are collected under suitable headings;
(2) General overheads which apply to the whole undertaking are divided among the departments, both service and production;
(3) The service department costs are shared among production departments (usually only cutting and one or more sewing rooms) on a suitable basis. For instance, personnel costs may be shared according to the number of people employed, maintenance costs

according to the number or value of machines, production planning costs according to the quantity of output.
(4) The total production department overhead is absorbed or recovered by making a charge against each garment which passes through the department.

Three methods of absorbing overheads are used in garment manufacture. The simplest is a rate per garment. This method divides the total overhead by the number of garments to be produced. It is accurate only when, rarely, the styles produced all have a similar work content. Otherwise high work content garments carry less than their due share of the overhead burden, low work content garments more. The other methods are a percentage added to the cost of direct wages, and a rate per standard direct labour hour. When, in process costing, accumulation of labour costs and averaging takes place weekly, these two methods produce the same effect.

For example, if the total overhead over a 30 week season is £648 000, the overhead to be absorbed each week is £21 600. Thus 150 per cent is added each week to the total direct labour cost of £14 400; or the overhead is absorbed at the rate of £5.625 per standard hour. Style B at 20 standard minutes or a budget labour cost of £1.25 attracts an overhead of £1.875.

Marginal costing

The approach to costing outlined so far is known as absorption costing because all costs, including fixed costs, are completely absorbed into the total cost of the garment. Fixed costs are costs of time because they accumulate with the passage of time. Fixed may not be fixed in amount, because the price of services changes, but the significant point is that they do not change with changes in the volume of output. The company must pay these expenses even if output fluctuates. Lower

Table 7.4 Absorption costings.

	Style (£)		
	A	B	C
Material cost	4.312	4.875	4.656
Direct labour cost	1.875	1.250	0.938
Total overhead	2.813	1.875	1.406
Total cost	9.000	8.000	7.000
Selling price	11.25	10.00	8.75

Table 7.5 Marginal costings (assume 90 per cent of overhead is fixed).

	Style (£)		
	A	B	C
Material cost	4.312	4.875	4.656
Direct labour cost	1.875	1.250	0.938
Total variable overhead	0.281	0.188	0.141
Total marginal cost	6.468	6.313	5.735
Contribution	4.782	3.687	3.015
Selling price	11.25	10.00	8.75

output means fixed overheads are under-recovered and hence must be paid out of profit; higher output means that fixed overheads are recovered by the budget output and the extra output provides not only the expected profit, but that part of the overhead absorption rate which covers fixed overheads is also profit.

In marginal costing, however, overheads are divided into two categories, although not necessarily directly: fixed overheads (i.e. those that do not change with output) and variable overheads (i.e. those which do vary with output, such as electricity). Only variable overheads are apportioned and then absorbed as a percentage added to wages or a rate per direct labour hour. Fixed overheads are recovered from the *contribution* which is left when total marginal costs are subtracted from sales revenue.

It is obvious that for a given output and sales the total profit remains the same for both absorption costing and marginal costing. They are only different ways of handling the same set of figures.

What is useful is the idea of *contribution to fixed overhead and profit*. When a company is considering a number of probable levels of output during the development of a sales/production plan, it is not just tedious to recalculate a new absorption rate for every level of output, but to calculate total contribution for each level connects the activity directly with profit, for:

Total profit = contribution − fixed overheads

If a company cannot sell all its output at regular prices, it may take a lower priced sale order. Marginal cost indicates the level below which the selling price should not fall. The contribution will be nil and the overall profit will be lower, but by selling at a lower price the company keeps the factory going at full output and maintains its labour force, whose skill is the basis of future profits.

Table 7.6   A simple view of profit.

| | Style (£) | | |
	A	B	C
Material cost	4.312	4.875	4.656
Direct labour cost	1.875	1.250	0.938
Total overhead (@ 150%)	2.813	1.875	1.406
Total cost	9.000	8.000	7.000
Selling price	11.25	10.00	8.75
Gross profit	2.25	2.00	1.75

Table 7.7   Contribution per labour hour.

| | Style | | |
	A	B	C
Selling price	£11.25	£10.00	£8.75
Marginal cost	£6.47	£6.31	£5.74
Contribution (selling price marginal cost)	£4.78	£3.69	£3.01
Sewing room labour hours	0.5	0.33	0.25
Contribution per labour hour	£9.56	£11.07	£12.04

Table 7.8   Profit yield for each style.

Style	Total contribution		Fixed overhead		Profit
A yields 3840 × £9.56 =	£36 710	less	£19 440	=	£17 280
B yields 3840 × £11.07 =	£42 509	less	£19 440	=	£23 069
C yields 3840 × £12.04 =	£46 234	less	£19 440	=	£26 794

The idea of contribution can be extended in the sense of *contribution per labour hour*. The limiting resource of a clothing manufacturer is sewing room labour; what the operators in the sewing room can produce is what the company can produce and sell. Hence the analysis of contribution in terms of sewing room labour can be crucial to a company's profitability.

Table 7.6 shows the three style examples used in the analysis of labour cost. So far the analysis shows a satisfactory picture, because all styles yield a gross profit of 20 per cent. But Table 7.7 shows a different picture in terms of contribution per labour hour. The sewing

Table 7.9 Analysis of agreed contribution per labour hour.

	Style	
	A	B
Marginal cost	£6.47	£6.31
Sewing room labour hours	0.5	0.33
Contribution per labour hour	£6.02	£4.01
Selling price	£12.49	£10.32

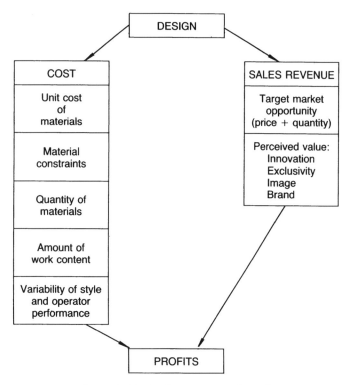

Fig. 7.6 Designing: costs and profits.

room capacity is 3840 standard hours of output per week, and the yields are shown in Table 7.8.

The concept of contribution per labour hour can be used in a number of ways:

(1) To identify garment styles with a low or high contribution per labour hour.

(2)   To calculate prices yielding an agreed contribution per labour hour. Suppose the contribution of £12.04 per hour achieved by Style C were applied to the other two, the result would be as shown in Table 7.9. This price may be too high to meet the competition in the market place or the requirements of the retail customer. Hence market conditions will impose a varying contribution rate if the manufacturer is to offer the full and varied range of styles which customers expect.

(3)   To evaluate future proposals in the light of their predicted contribution rate.

(4)   To encourage sales of high contribution styles by paying commission to representatives at a rate varying directly with the contribution per labour hour.

(5)   To identify customers who buy garments with a high contribution rate.

The point of this chapter is to emphasise that almost every choice the designer makes changes the price and cost of the garments (Fig. 7.6). The price comes from the precise point in the market the designer chooses to attack, and the perceived value of the garments. Cost changes arise from the demands which the designer makes on fabric and work content, in both crude and subtle ways as outlined in this chapter; and from how the volume sold affects overhead recovery, the third major element of cost.

8

Costs of Product Development

The aim of this chapter is to analyse the costs and benefits of the process of product development.

Analysis of design costs

Employing a designer

The total cost of employing a designer is considerably more than paying a salary. It includes the additional social costs of employment such as social security, pension and perhaps health insurance. A designer may also be expected to have the extensive travel costs of attending fashion shows and symposia wherever they take place. The costs of providing a working environment include costs of space, depreciation on the equipment provided and the costs of consumables. The size of the bill depends on the size of the company, the status of the designer and the designer's job definition.

Design concepts

The output of a designer (in the conventional sense) is a series of design concepts in the form of sketches, either presented individually or as part of a story. The average cost of a design concept in a form which can progress down the chain of product development is clearly expressed by the total cost of employing a designer divided by the quantity of design concepts produced. This will vary according to the complexity of the design concept, the level of innovation and the methods used.

Cost per sample

From the continuous stream of design ideas emanating from the designers, only some will be selected for further development. Hence it is useful to establish a *ratio of design sketch produced to first sample made*. Multiplying this ratio by the average cost per design concept produces the average design cost per sample.

Prototype pattern

The total cost of employing a pattern cutter includes elements similar to that of the designer. Pay and travel expenses are likely to be lower, but the cost of consumables higher in some circumstances. Hence the cost of a prototype pattern is expressed by the total cost of employing a pattern cutter divided by the quantity of prototype patterns produced.

Producing a sample

The cost of producing a sample can be analysed under the conventional headings of material cost, labour cost and overheads. The material cost is the cost of fabric and trims purchased, the labour cost is the cost of the sample machinists employed divided by the number of samples produced, and the overheads are the costs of space incurred and the cost of supplying services to the sample room. Adding together the design cost per sample, the cost of a prototype pattern and the cost of producing a sample gives the total cost of producing a first sample.

Producing a production pattern

Again, from the first samples submitted to a range meeting only some will be selected for further development through production patterns and grading. Hence it is useful to establish a *ratio of first sample to graded production patterns*. Further development may also include alteration to the methods used to make the sample, alterations to the patterns and adaptation of the design concept, in order to solve technical, commercial or aesthetic problems.

The cost of producing a production pattern and grading the range of sizes can be found in the same way as the cost of producing a sample above. It will vary according to whether manual or computer based methods are used.

The *average total cost of a set of graded production patterns* will be found first by multiplying the ratio of first sample to graded production patterns by the total cost of producing a first sample, and then adding the cost of producing a production pattern and grading.

Development costs in the factory

Development costs in the factory include two major elements: adaptations to the manufacturing process and training of operators.

Adaptations to the manufacturing process may be as simple as templates or markers to achieve accurate positioning of features such as buttonholes or pockets. They may involve the purchase or manufacture of specialised guides or machine feet or feeds to cope with specialised features such as piping or lace. Finally, a new style may entail the purchase of specialised machinery for, say, pin tucking, saddle stitching or joining elasticated parts – a considerable capital investment.

Capital investment decisions on a large scale are the subject of considerable mathematical analysis, using net present value or discounted cash flow (DCF) techniques. At the level of sewing machinery purchase the simpler technique of payback period is frequently enough. The question to be answered is how long will it be before the additional income generated pays for the cost of the machine installed. The extra income may be in the form of reduction in labour cost, in comparison with former more labour intensive methods, or an increased contribution to fixed overheads and profit generated by the style for which the machinery was purchased. In the latter, the capital cost may have to be amortised over the life of that style. In simple terms, a machine costing £2000 to install to manufacture 4000 of a style will add 50p per garment to the cost of that style. Hence the aim of designers may be to create further styles which make use of the machine. In a sense the machine itself inspires further designs, and these also provide a lower level of amortisation of the machine cost.

The cost of retraining operators depends on the planned output of new styles and the number who will be retrained, the level of flexibility in the skills of the operators based on the objectives of their initial training, and the amount of innovation in the new styles. How much of this cost of training and retraining can be separated will depend on the level of sophistication of production management and the need to attach varying training costs to individual styles.

Almost every element in the above analysis is variable in itself and in its effect. For instance, a designer may produce fewer design concepts but may have a higher than average proportion accepted for sampling, or the designer may have a lower proportion accepted at that stage but a higher proportion accepted at the range meeting. In other words the average total cost of a graded set of production patterns will vary for each designer according to performance at all stages.

Style or product profitability

It is possible to summarise design costs and their effect by analysing style or product profitability, as in Table 8.1.

Table 8.1 Style or product profitability.

	Sales (garment units) and style					
	1000X		500Y		2000Z	
	Per garment (£)	Total (£)	Per garment (£)	Total (£)	Per garment (£)	Total (£)
Sales revenue	20	20 000	30	15 000	15	30 000
Cost of sales:						
Direct material	8	8 000	18	9 000	6	12 000
Direct labour	4	4 000	3	1 500	4	8 000
Prime cost	12	12 000	21.0	10 500	10	20 000
Variable overhead	1	1 000	0.75	375	1	2 000
Marginal cost	13	13 000	21.75	10 875	11	22 000
Total contribution	7	7 000	8.25	4 125	4	8 000
Fixed costs:						
Production, selling, overhead etc.*		4 000		1 500		8 000
Costs incurred by design and product development		1 000		1 500		500
Total fixed costs		5 000		3 000		8 500
Profit (or loss) on sales		2 000		1 125		(500)
Profit (or loss) (%)		10		7.5		(1.66)

* Fixed costs of production and sales etc. are charged at 100 per cent of direct labour.

Assume Style X achieves target profit.

Style Y achieves a lower profit because of higher design costs in proportion to sales. It also has high material costs, perhaps not subject to critical examination by the design team. It has the potential to achieve good profitability because of a high contribution per unit of labour cost (per direct labour hour).

Style Z achieves an overall loss because of high labour costs. It has much lower design costs, perhaps indicating sloppy designing. Had labour costs been, say, 20% of selling price as with Style X, they would have been £3 per garment and £6000 in total, with a fixed overhead charge of £3 per garment and £6000 in total. Total costs would have been £4000 lower and profit £3500; in other words with proper design and product development Style Z is potentially the most profitable style.

Profits of design

The profits of design have five elements:

(1) Sales volume per style launched, or price per garment multiplied by the volume sold;
(2) Percentage gross contribution to fixed overheads and profit for each style;
(3) Actual contribution for each style;
(4) Number of styles launched from each designer's output;
(5) Contribution to fixed overhead and profit from each designer.

Contribution may be increased by increasing the volume of sales from a style. It may also increase through the design of styles with high perceived value and hence high contribution in relation to total marginal cost, or with a high contribution per direct labour hour. A designer may increase contribution by having more styles launched. All these add up to the total contribution arising from the work of a designer. It is therefore possible to make financial judgements about the work of individual designers.

Example of design costs and profits

The following is an example of the cost and profit analysis outlined in this chapter.

Costs

(1)	Total cost of employing a designer	£30 000
(2)	Number of design concepts produced	200
(3)	Cost per design concept	£150 (£30 000 ÷ 200)
(4)	Design concept/first sample ratio	3 : 1
(5)	Design cost per sample	£450 (3 × £150)
(6)	Cost of prototype pattern	£100
(7)	Cost of manufacturing first sample	£100

(8) Total cost of first sample £650 (£450 + £100 + £100)
(9) Ratio of first sample to set of 2:1
     graded patterns
(10) Cost of production pattern £25
     and grading
(11) Total cost of a set of graded £1 325 (£650 × 2 + £25)
     patterns
(12) Development costs in the £1 000
     factory

Profits

(1) Sales volume per style launched £40 000
(2) Percentage contribution for each style 30
(3) Actual contribution for each style £12 000
(4) Number of styles launched 33
(5) Total contribution from a designer £400 000

The total design costs in this example are found by adding together items (11) and (12) above and multiplying by the number of styles launched, that is £2325 by 33 or £76 725. It is not possible to speculate what profit is left from the remaining contribution of £323 275, when design costs are subtracted from the designer's total contribution, because the level of fixed costs cannot be known in this example.

9

Operations Management

This chapter describes the function of production planning and control, the organisation for production, and their relationship to design.

Flows of information

This section describes the activities of production planning and control, which translate sales orders and sales forecasts into deliveries to customers. The control which makes or breaks a company's delivery schedule is the marrying of fabric and trimmings deliveries to available production capacity at the right time. Delivery on time represents the most important service the company offers to its customers. The customer expects delivery of garments to fit in with in-store promotions, local advertising, new season launches and making space available to accommodate new garments. Successive failures to deliver on time are the most common cause of retail stores dropping a manufacturer and seeking more reliable sources of supply. Many causes of late delivery originate in failures of production, but designers' mistakes in planning and their indecisiveness can be worse. A late pattern change when the fabric is already spread, a change in measurement specification, the discovery that a fabric frays excessively or the dye bleeds on to the press covers, or the choice of a button so esoteric that supply cannot be guaranteed in sufficient quantity at a late stage, are all essentially failures of design.

The production planning and control department collects and gives out information and decisions to other departments in a clothing manufacturing company: design, marketing, buying, manufacturing, personnel and cost accounts.

In relation to design the department records the ordering and delivery of sample lengths of fabric, predicts material and labour costs and estimates delivery schedules for the different styles in preparation for range meetings, registers the decisions of range meetings, calculates the investment in machinery and training, and collects and issues specifications.

In relation to marketing the department assesses the capacity available for next season for manufacturing the types of garment in its plan. It also obtains from marketing an estimate of sales requirements, broken down into such categories as type (e.g. dress, blouse, skirt), style, fabric and delivery times. The company does not of course make these two assessments in isolation, for they are one and the same plan. To make what cannot be sold or to try and sell what cannot be made is the road to bankruptcy. The two assessments form the basis of a continuous dialogue between marketing and manufacturing, which at an agreed time hardens into the sales/production plan for the coming season. Production planning may have to temper both the optimism of a marketing department in the face of a new style range and the conservatism of production managers who have to make them.

During the operation of the plan, production planning and control will inform marketing regularly on actual production against the plan, in detail so that it may schedule deliveries to customers, and overall so that the company may adapt its sales plans (or production plans) in the face of under or over production.

The department informs the buying department of the requirements in fabric and trimmings for next season, in suitable categories: fabric for dresses, blouses or skirts, and within these categories fabrics for various stories or promotions, as well as delivery dates.

During the season, production planning and control will obtain details of stocks and orders in order to issue a regular control statement of the overall fabric and trimmings position, showing quantities still to buy or surpluses still to sell. In addition it will require the latest information on delivery dates for every individual cloth number in order that cutting dockets may be written when fabric is available.

In relation to manufacturing the department determines the making time for all styles – information essential in planning the use of manufacturing capacity and in predicting labour costs. It also determines the material content of all styles so that buying requirements may be estimated and material cost predicted (see Chapter 7). It publishes specifications for all styles in the coming season, and makes a schedule for cutting patterns and grading in the light of manufacturing schedules. It calculates the capacity of the sewing rooms, in garment units or standard time, to provide marketing with its estimate of available production and to assess labour requirements. It also draws up a detailed production budget (see Chapter 7) which predicts what the factory will produce, how many attendance hours it will need and how much it will cost.

During the season, production planning and control will determine the input to the cutting room and sewing room, will monitor output, actual labour strength (which is the basis of output), actual labour cost, actual fabric usage and work in progress (which controls throughput time), and will control the progressing of individual orders to ensure they are made in the correct sequence to meet agreed delivery dates.

In relation to personnel the department sets out the season's labour requirements for achieving the production budget. It monitors actual recruitment or staff reduction to stimulate faster recruitment or redundancy where appropriate. It also ensures that enough training capacity is provided to meet the needs of the production plan.

In relation to cost accounts, production planning and control provides standard times and material estimates for all styles so that direct costs can be calculated.

Levelling

Levelling is a persistent problem for many clothing manufacturers. The problem lies in the difference between delivery requirements and production requirements; delivery is concentrated into short periods whereas production is usually continuous. In menswear, deliveries of topcoats tend to be at a maximum in the months of September, October and November. Most swimwear deliveries take place from March to May. When a company owns and manages its own factories, it does its reputation in the labour market no good to hire and fire staff to meet production at times of high delivery. In addition it recognises that its staff embody the skill required to manufacture its garments, an asset which would waste away if it did not provide continuous employment. Manufacturers find a number of ways of levelling.

The first is quite simply to produce early and hold stocks until the time for delivery arrives. Suppose that the delivery requirements for topcoats for September, October and November are 3900 a month, but average only 700 a month for the remaining nine months of the year, making an annual total of 18 000. To level production results in a monthly output of 1500. If it is assumed that the company has delivered all orders by the end of November in one year and has no stock left (an unlikely assumption), then in each succeeding month up to August the following year the company will be manufacturing 800 more topcoats than are required for immediate delivery. The stock will stand at the end of August at 7200, which will reduce to 4800 at the end of September, 2400 at the end of October and nil at the end of November. This means the average stock would be 3600, which represents over two months' output. If the average total cost of each topcoat were £100, this would represent an average amount of £360 000 tied up in topcoat stock. The cost of having to provide this amount of extra working capital, much higher at one time of the year, plus the opportunities missed by not having it available elsewhere, may well make this answer to the levelling problem uneconomic.

Another answer is to introduce other products or styles into the range to take up the production slack outside periods of peak delivery. The other products must be able to fill unused capacity efficiently. In the topcoat example an alternative range might be sports jackets or rainwear. For swimwear the alternative might be dresses. However, this solution produces another set of costs. Staff must be retrained twice a year to cope with the alternatives. Wage costs will remain at or near average and weekly total overhead is the same, while output is lower during the learning periods. In addition the company will bear the extra overhead costs of designing and developing a full additional range.

A third answer, especially in metropolitan fashion markets, is sub-contracting. Here the entrepreneur designs the range and markets it, buys the cloth and delivers to customers, but sub-contracts the manufacturing to outworkers. This means that the outworker does not have to organise a sophisticated marketing and planning operation, and it provides elasticity of manufacturing for the entrepreneur who is operating among a network, consisting perhaps of chains of sub-contractors, for whom he has no direct responsibility. Clearly, in the relationship with the main outworkers, there is a large degree of mutual dependence, but the more sub-contracting moves down the chain away from the entrepreneur making the decisions, the less influence the sub-contracting manufacturer has on those decisions. Perhaps only in these conditions of great flexibility can a metropolitan fashion market operate efficiently.

Example season

A sequence of events during the planning and operation of a season might be like the following example. The company orders sample lengths at the end of November and delivers between mid-May and the end of October for the winter season the following year. The company carries up to 100 styles per season and manufactures several thousand garments using outworkers (see Fig. 9.1).

Sample lengths ordered

The designer buys sample lengths of fabric, usually at Interstoff, the international trade fair.

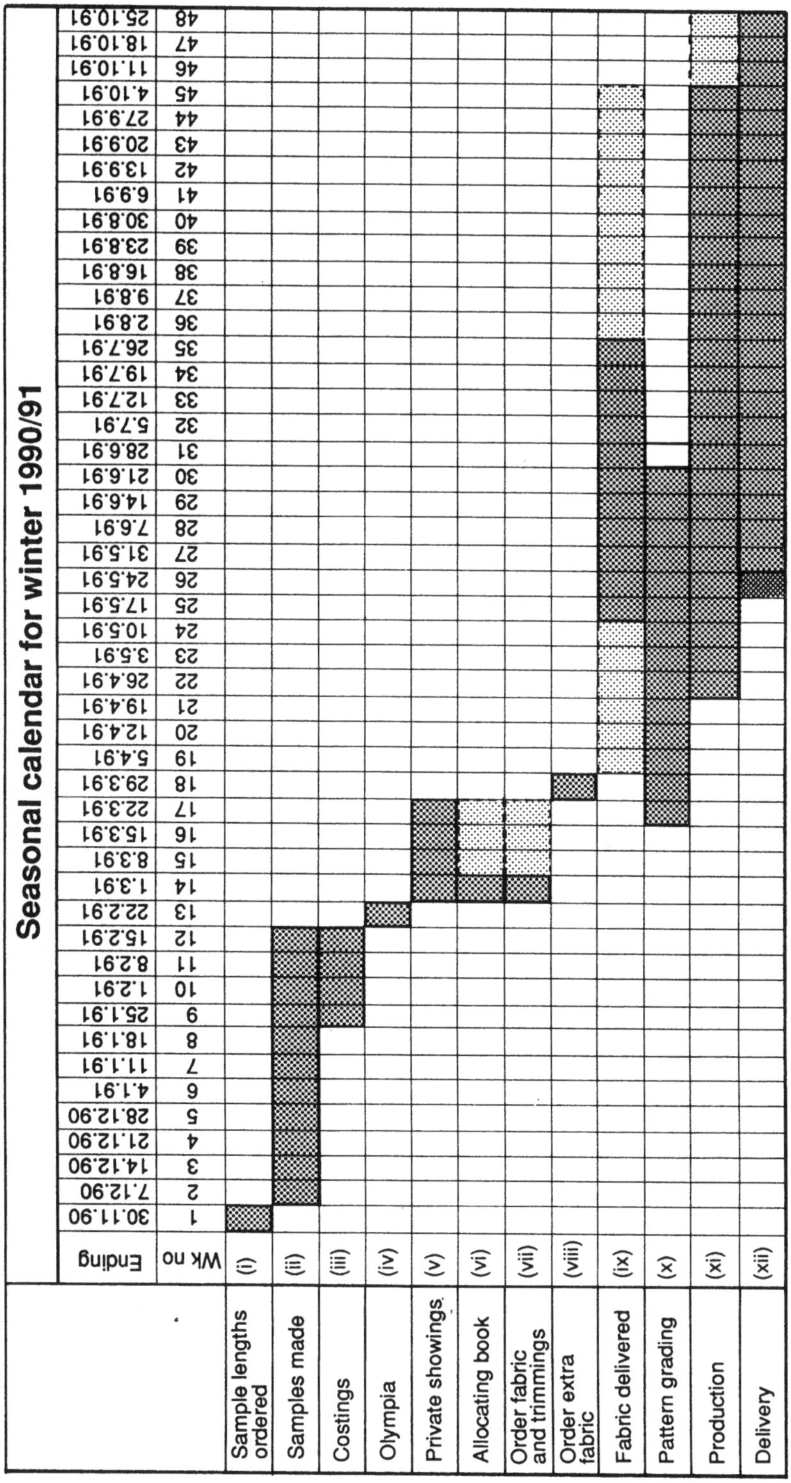

Seasonal calendar for winter 1990/91

Wk no	Ending
1	30.11.90
2	7.12.90
3	14.12.90
4	21.12.90
5	28.12.90
6	4.1.91
7	11.1.91
8	18.1.91
9	25.1.91
10	1.2.91
11	8.2.91
12	15.2.91
13	22.2.91
14	1.3.91
15	8.3.91
16	15.3.91
17	22.3.91
18	29.3.91
19	5.4.91
20	12.4.91
21	19.4.91
22	26.4.91
23	3.5.91
24	10.5.91
25	17.5.91
26	24.5.91
27	31.5.91
28	7.6.91
29	14.6.91
30	21.6.91
31	28.6.91
32	5.7.91
33	12.7.91
34	19.7.91
35	26.7.91
36	2.8.91
37	9.8.91
38	16.8.91
39	23.8.91
40	30.8.91
41	6.9.91
42	13.9.91
43	20.9.91
44	27.9.91
45	4.10.91
46	11.10.91
47	18.10.91
48	25.10.91

Activities:

(i) Sample lengths ordered
(ii) Samples made
(iii) Costings
(iv) Olympia
(v) Private showings
(vi) Allocating book
(vii) Order fabric and trimmings
(viii) Order extra fabric
(ix) Fabric delivered
(x) Pattern grading
(xi) Production
(xii) Delivery

Fig. 9.1 Seasonal calendar.

Samples

The designer designs a collection of up to 100 garments, in 'story' groups of fabric. The pattern cutter cuts first patterns. Samples are made in the company's sample room on the premises.

Costings

The pattern cutter makes a marker for a single garment and records the quantity of fabric(s) used for each style. The production manager establishes a making price for each style. The accountant calculates a total cost for each style.

Olympia

The collection is presented at the Olympia fashion show to international buyers. About half the total capacity is sold during the four days of the show.

Private showings

British customers visit the company for individual showings of the collection.

Allocation book

Individual customers' orders are collated under styles to form a production order for each style, showing total quantities in each size and colour and estimated delivery dates.

Order fabric

An estimate of the fabric required is made from the initial orders at Olympia. Quantities of fabric are reserved and confirmed when all garment orders are in.

Order trimmings

The company uses the same method for ordering trimmings as for ordering fabrics. The importance of this lies in the fact that in many styles the trims, such as embroidered panels, are a significant feature of the style. This illustrates the influence of design on the buying activity.

Fabric delivered

There are two categories of fabric:

(1) Standards, which are readily available, such as velvet and wool crêpe. Delivery is usually within one month of placing an order.

(2) Specials, which are imported fabrics, special prints, sequinned fabrics and silk screen prints. Delivery is anything from two to five months. Again it is the design function which selects fabrics with long delivery dates.

Grading

The pattern cutter makes a production pattern, including seams, notches and so on, using pattern card. Grading goes to a sub-contractor.

Production

When fabric is available it is sent with the graded patterns to outworkers, who cut, make and press the garments. Completed garments are returned to the company for inspection. Lead times vary according to the quantities required.

Delivery

When accepted, garments are recorded in the stock book and stored until despatch.

The process is controlled through a series of forms:

(1) The design sketch goes to the pattern cutter with the costings sheet.
(2) The pattern cutter fills in, on the costing sheet, details related to the style and quantities of fabric used, with material estimates for both single and multiple lays, accessories and labels. Two copies go to the production department, who provide the make price, retaining one copy and sending the other to the accountant, who calculates total cost. This costing sheet is created for each model (see Fig. 9.2).
(3) Each salesperson carries a price list, with style number, description, prices, constraints on possible variations, size range offered, earliest fabric delivery and earliest garment delivery.
(4) The cloth delivery control sheet shows the following events on a time scale for each individual fabric:

- Projected delivery date of fabric;
- Confirmation of delivery dates;
- A reminder to supplier one month before delivery;
- New delivery dates if necessary;
- Invoice received;
- Whole or part delivery of fabric.

Costing sheet							Serial no. *2250*		
Style no. *85*		Type					Date		
Description *Long Evening Dress*									
W *Wholesale Price*		S *Retail Price*					Customer name		
Outworker							Order no.		
Labels			Belt				Swatches		
Large 100% Viscose 100% Silk 100% Acetate (F) Dry Clean Only			None						*2449* Black Velvet *1715* Pink Taffeta *2542* Purple Taffeta
Position	Description	Supplier	Stock no.	Width m.	Price	Costing for 1	Costing for	Net price	
Material	Black Velvet		2449	120 CM	£7.23	2.20M	7.50M		
Material coat	Pink Taffeta		1715	90 CM	£6.00	3.10M			
Lining	Black Milor		1848	90 CM	£0.84	3.00M			
Lining	Pink Organza		2589	105 CM	£2.50	2.30M			
Boning				1 CM	£0.16	1.70M			
Boning Ribbon				250 MM	£0.13	1.80M			
Hang Ribbon				5 MM	£0.008	0.80M			
Cotton					£0.35	1			
Hook & Eye					£0.01	1			
Weight *820 gms*						Sundries			
						Subtotal			
						Make price			
						Cost			

Fig. 9.2 Costing sheet.

Cloth delivery control sheet											Season	Winter 1990/91			
					Metres ordered for delivery										
Stock No.	Supplier and description	April		May		June		July		Aug		Sept		Oct	
		-15	-30	-15	-30	-15	-30	-15	-30	-15	-30	-15	-30	-15	-30
2449	Black Velvet			250		Ordered For Nxt Mnth									
						250 5.6		Confirmed For Time 6							
						250 x5.6		Reminder Supplier							
						250 x5.6	(250) x20.6	New Delivery Date Confirmed							
							(250) x20.6 ✓	Invoice Received							
							(250) x20.6 50	Part Delivery							
							(250) x20.6 50	Delivery Completed							
						250 x5.6	(250) x20.6 50								

Fig. 9.3 Cloth delivery control sheet.

Cloth record chart

Stock no.	2449
Width	120CM
Fibre content	100% Viscose
Supplier	
Description	Black Velvet
Cost	£7.25/
Swatch	

Sales / Cloth required

Style no.	Qty. m.	Del.	Costing m.	Total m.	Cumul. m.
85	2	May	2	4	4
	5	July	2	10	14
	10	Aug	2	20	34
	5	Sept	2	10	44
	9	Oct	2	18	66

Purchase orders

Date	Qty. m.	Balance to deliver	Del. date request	Confirmed Date	For	Date
25.2.90	250	50	May	5.5	206	20.6.90

Cloth usage

Stock m.	Dkt. no.	Style no.	Used m.	Stock m.
200	2220	85	113	87

Usage continued

Date	Stock m.	Dkt. no.	Style no.	Used m.	Stock m.

Fig. 9.4 Cloth record chart.

Order

Date _____ 18th March 1990

Name _____

Address _____

Terms: 20th to 19th payable on the following 10th less 2½%
No returns accepted or claims allowed after 7 days from date of invoice

Style	Description	Colour US / UK	6 / 8	8 / 10	10 / 12	12 / 14	14 / 16	Price
85	Velvet Long Evening Dress	Black/Pink						Wholesale
	Slash & CN, Starter At Top	Black/Purple			1	1		Price

Commence from _____ Ex. Factory May 31st. 1990

English law prevails on all orders

Fig. 9.5 Customer's order.

The example in Fig. 9.3 shows an order for 250 metres of black velvet for initial delivery in mid-May. The order is confirmed for 5 June. After a reminder the supplier moves delivery to 20 June. After receiving the invoice, part of the order is delivered on 20 June and the residue on 26 June. The example in Fig. 9.3 shows each event on a separate line; in practice all the entries for a fabric number would be shown on one line, as in the last line of the example. This type of form keeps up to date with changes, keeps up pressure on the supplier and provides information on the reliability of suppliers.

(5) There is a cloth record card for each fabric (Fig. 9.4). The form is in three sections: the first lists sales cumulatively; the second summarises the ordering and delivery of fabric; the third is a record of how the fabric is used. Both the stockroom and the sales office are kept aware of quantities still to be sold.

(6) Confirmation of customers' orders (Fig. 9.5) involves three copies; one to the customer, one to the production department for the allocating book and one as a record in the sales office.

(7) In the allocating book customers' orders are collated by style, rated in order of delivery priority and numbered in sequence.

(8) Dockets are written instructions to customers giving style, quantities in each size, fabric and trim details and labels.

(9) The style progress chart is shown in Fig. 9.6. At the left is a description of the style, the date the pattern was graded, the date the docket was issued to the outworker and the date the first repeat was approved. On the right are the last dates by which garments should be received from the outworker. One week is allowed in house for inspecting, registering and packing garments before despatch. These charts enable the production manager to inform the outworkers what garments are required in advance of the dates, to keep pressure on the outworkers and to reallocate work if an outworker cannot meet the dates.

(10) The outworker's delivery note gives details of garments delivered.

(11) In the stock book garments are registered and given a stock number, remaining in the book until despatched. They are also recorded on the retained copy of the customer's order, in the allocating book against the customer with the highest priority and on the copy of the docket in the production department.

(12) The delivery note goes with orders when despatched, with copies to the three places listed in (11).

This control system reflects the need for accurate information, continuously updated, especially about fabric deliveries and

Style progress chart

Season: Winter 1990–91   Outworker:

Style no.	Description	Pattern graded	Fabric delivered	Docket written	1st. repeat approved	Minimum no. required by					
						May 24	June 21	July 26	Aug 23	Sept 20	Oct 19
85	Black Velvet Evening Dress Pink Taffeta Sash	12/1.90	25.6.90	22.90	16.5.90	$\frac{1}{14}$		$\frac{1}{8}\ \frac{1}{10}\ \frac{1}{12}\ \frac{2}{24}$	$\frac{1}{8}\ \frac{3}{10}\ \frac{4}{12}\ \frac{2}{14}$	$\frac{1}{8}\ \frac{4}{12}$	$\frac{2}{10}\ \frac{6}{12}\ \frac{1}{14}$
85	Purple Taffeta Sash	12/1.90	25.6.90	22.90	16.5.90	$\frac{1}{14}$					

Fig. 9.6 Style progress chart.

outworkers' output, neither of which are under the direct authority of the company.

Production organisation

Operations are divisions of the total work content of garments. Each operation consists of a work cycle which is the sequence of elements of cutting, sewing, fusing or pressing required to perform a job or yield a unit of production. Operations define the work done by people in a factory. In the sewing room, the breakdown of the total work content of the garment into long, medium or short operations is influenced by the amount of work content in the garment, by the expected quantity of output of an individual style and by the number employed in the company manufacturing it, with the consequent potential for specialisation among its operators and managers. Thus a high work content garment manufactured as individual garments in a small company will tend to have long operations, if not a form of 'make-through' organisation where an operator constructs the majority of the garment herself. The operation length is likely to be short for a low work content garment, such as briefs, manufactured continuously in a large company, with specialist managers as industrial engineers who can plan for the best utilisation of people and machinery. Operations can vary from perhaps hours for a hand-made bespoke jacket to fractions of a minute in the bulk production of briefs. Between the two extremes lies every possible variation.

Six factors influence the planning of sewing room organisations:

(1) The building itself and the requirements for safety constrain the layout.
(2) The degree of specialisation or the division into small or large operations is determined in the way outlined above.
(3) Pareto's principle, which has been applied in stock control for many years, appears to apply equally well in the sewing room. It is sometimes known as the 80−20 rule: 80 per cent of the volume comes from only 20 per cent of the styles. Indeed some companies establish a cut-off point and refuse to run styles which do not sell a certain minimum quantity.
(4) The need for maximum utilisation of labour. Traditionally this has meant maintaining a sufficient level of work in progress in the form of buffer stocks at individual operations, to reduce the likelihood of operators running out of work because of variations in pace among those before them in the production line.
(5) The garment itself which leads to the design of the process of manufacture. This forms the basis of the series of operations in

the sewing room and their work content is measured by their standard times. The type of garment also strongly influences the stitch types selected and the basic machinery used in the operations. Designers not only design the garment but also, in varying degrees, play a part in the design of the process of manufacture. If the designer is to have complete confidence that the manufacturing process is capable of reproducing the design concept accurately, with the right quality and at the designed cost, then he or she may veto or demand the purchase of certain machinery, the use of certain types of trims and the installation of certain methods used by operators. The designer may insist on additional work content with the object of safeguarding quality. Menswear designers, concerned with a tailored garment, take a particular interest in pressing because this plays such an important part in the achievement of shape.

(6) The market works in three ways:

   (a) The interaction of the company and the market determines the total volume of a style which is sold.

   (b) The market influences delivery policy. Garments with a high fashion content generally demand shorter delivery schedules than staple garments so that they are on the market while customers still wish to buy. Shorter delivery schedules mean a lower level of work in progress.

   (c) The market influences the variability of the product. The clothing industry as a whole produces a range of garments from shirts (although variety in that sector has increased over the years) and some types of work clothing, through men's suits where a basic chassis carries variable features, to women's dresses where a large number of styles show not only variability of feature but also different sequences of assembly. The significant indices are the average number of styles at any one time in the mix fed to the sewing room, and the total number of styles over a period such as a year or a season. Clearly the designer serves the market by providing the number of styles the market requires, but it is legitimate to ask the question how often a failure of conviction leads to 'overkill'.

Style

Here it is useful to define the term style. To a designer or salesman a style is often a shape, a silhouette, a total effect. To a production manager a style is a collection of individual features making up a garment. Thus the designer's 'style' may comprise several of the production manager's 'styles'.

The precise way in which style hits the sewing room breaks down into:

- varying sequences of operations, a concept at the root of planning;
- varying times for operations in the same basic sequence, which does not affect the sewing room nearly so radically;
- varying fabrics for the same basic garment, which might demand changes in the sewing mechanism or several machines on the same operation.

Make through

Two sorts of organisation have been common traditionally. The first is so-called 'make through'. This is, for instance, carried out by skilled tailors who make the shell of the jacket, or by machinists who perform all the operations on a dress except pressing and certain special machining. It is commonly used in smaller sewing rooms in the older clothing manufacturing centres. The operator exhibits high skill in relation to knowledge and technique, but lower speed skills. Sewing room managers will use make through in low volume production, very specialised quality demands, high variety and the availability of traditionally trained garment skills. It is important to note that in a sense 'make through' is a misnomer, for the operator does not perform all the work in the garment. The make through operator carries out the main construction operation but, before and after this, lesser skilled operators do preparatory and finishing work such as overlocking, buttonholing and pressing.

Progressive bundle unit

The second sort of organisation is the so-called 'progressive bundle unit'. Here the operations are laid out logically according to the sequence of manufacturing for one garment style. The required number of operators for an approximate balance is allocated to each operation. There is sufficient storage space, in one form or another, for at least a moderate amount of work in progress to act as a buffer between the operations. The supervisor has both opportunity and responsibility to achieve line balance and attain the best level of production. The level of work in progress ensures that the operator is in command of her own output, giving the best opportunity for the application of individual incentive payment systems.

To these types of organisation must now be added two answers to the current demand for 'Quick Response': the Unit Production System and the Toyota Sewing System.

Unit Production System (UPS)

The UPS is based on a method of materials handling which has been available for over 20 years. It was formerly known as powered rail selector. It consists of a power driven loop with the workplaces spaced at regular intervals on the outside of it. Cut work is fed on to the line, a garment to each hanger, with perhaps baskets for small parts. After the garments are assembled they are transferred to hangers. Hangers are addressed to operations by a button system. On arrival the hanger is automatically diverted on to the storage line for the workplace. The operator sews the garment and addresses the hanger to its next operation, anywhere on the system. After the last operation the operator addresses the hanger to the feed-off area.

The UPS applies computer technology to this rail system. The computer memory contains comprehensive information about production resources: a list of all the operators, the operations they can do and the performance they can achieve. Details of the orders are fed into the computer: style, sequence of operations with standard times, quantity and delivery date. The programme then finds the best route through the system for that order and style, in order to meet the delivery date and make full use of operators. Succeeding orders, when fed in, may bring about an adjustment of the route of previous orders. The system's name stems from the fact that it handles single garments, not the traditional bundles. It keeps track of the position of every garment in the system. This highlights a point that production managers were perhaps hardly aware of: that garment production is very information intensive. In the past it was impossible for production managers to keep track of the movement of every garment in the sewing room unless it was very small. Hence the need for a quantity of work in progress, to provide buffer stocks to prevent operators waiting for work. With all the variations of style, colour and size, and the capacity of the manager's and supervisors' memories, nothing less would work.

Given such comprehensive control by the computer, the need for a large quantity of work in progress in the sewing room is very much reduced. Some installations of a UPS have seen a reduction of work in progress and throughput time reduced from three weeks to eight hours. The first benefit of this is to the clothing pipeline as a whole. The buyer in the retail store can now make decisions about what to bring into the store from suppliers almost three weeks later – only a few days before it is required. Hence the buyer's decisions are more likely to be correct because the decision will take effect only a few days ahead, and there are likely to be fewer markdowns and stockouts. So potential profit is much greater. It is not therefore surprising to find that retail chain stores in the mid-1980s encouraged their suppliers to install UPS.

Whether the manufacturers alone would have installed the system is a difficult question; the benefit to the manufacturer is much less obvious, against a very high cost to install.

The Toyota Sewing System

The second answer to the need for Quick Response is a modular organisation – the Toyota Sewing System – so called from the company which first developed it. The most obvious characteristic of this system is that operators stand to work, which promotes rapid movement. The machines in use are raised to the correct height on pedestals and laid out in a U-shape. The operators are organised in small teams of eight to 10 and are each skilled in a group of operations which overlaps with the group of the adjacent operator; hence at least two operators can perform every operation. The operators have autonomy to decide how they will break up the operations on a new style, and who will do what. A supervisor is available to help with technical information. There is a considerable investment in training time while the team is being built up. The team works on only one bundle at a time; thus there is virtually no work in progress.

The production manager provides continuous feedback to the operators on their performance through an overhead display, showing target output and actual output at all times of the working day. Reported performances after training are at least as high as individuals in a progressive bundle unit. The motivation of members of the team is very strong, absenteeism is low and the team normally rejects a substitute if a member is away. Labour turnover is considerably reduced.

The success of the system rests on the social interactions and group dynamics of the team and the U-shaped line aids this communication. The workplace is the territory of the team and only designated project leaders and mechanics have right of access – managers by invitation only. Team meetings are held regularly to promote the exchange of information. An important objective is to bring different means of support to the operators so that they do not waste time searching for help. All machines under manual control have a maximum speed of 2500 stitches per minute. This results in less machine downtime, improved stitch quality and fewer maintenance requirements. The role of supervisor has been replaced by fewer section managers.

The Toyota Sewing System provides the same benefit to the clothing pipeline as the UPS, but the capital cost, while considerable, is very much less than that of the UPS. There appears to be one serious limitation to the use of the system: the total work content with which the team can cope. One suggestion is that the maximum work content is 10 standard minutes, but this is plainly too low. However, a 30 minute trouser or a 90 minute jacket would appear to be too high. The progressive bundle unit, for the moment, still has its day.

This chapter has related the work of the designer to operations management in the two areas of production planning and sewing room organisation. Design and production planning inter-relate at a number of points. Production planning should ensure the publication to all concerned of design decisions when they are made; provide information to design about projected costs at all stages of development and about actual costs of manufacture when these diverge from standard, and design modifications may be required; and schedule the manufacture of different styles between appropriate dates (besides scheduling the production of patterns and samples).

Design should comprehend the effect of a higher volume of styles during a season, the results flowing from late changes in design, the consequences of selecting a fabric with a long delivery time, and the difficulties that arise from designing an innovative garment with a longer than usual development time (patterns, folders on machines, training).

Design relates to the organisation of the sewing room for the most basic reason of all. It is here that the designer's garments are copied in their dozens, hundreds or thousands. Either the designer designs with this organisation in mind or finds the organisation inappropriate and seeks to change it within the possibilities available: level of specialisation of operations, flexibility, the ability to change style rapidly and quickness of response to the market. The factory is not simply that place which spoils the designer's garments but that place where the designer prevents the garments being spoiled.

Further Reading

This collection of books and articles will help the reader to follow up the themes in this book.

The bibliography on this subject is found in general collections of clothing sources. One of the oldest of these was produced by UNIDO (United Nations Industrial Development Organisation) (1974) *Information Sources on the Clothing Industry: Guides to Information Sources no. 12*, United Nations. A more recent collection is by H.C. Carr (Ed.) (1989) *Select Bibliography of Clothing Sources*, Emraine Publications, Ware. A useful list of titles from the United States Department of Commerce, Office of Textiles and Apparel is National Technical Information Service (NTIS) catalog of reports and material available from NTIS/US Department of Commerce, Springfield, Virginia 22161 in *Bobbin*, August 1982, Vol. 23, No. 12.

The best account of the running of a traditional clothing business is the book by Mischa Perlmutter (1944) *The Rag Bizness*, Wetzel Publishing, Los Angeles, written with a directness, simplicity and humour it would be hard to better. A revealing contrast is N. Alan Hunter (1990) *Quick Response in Apparel Manufacturing*, The Textile Institute, Manchester.

1 The process and structure of the industry

Reiner G. Stoll in Product Performance in the Sewn Products Industry, *Bobbin*, August 1969, 10 (12), looks at the clothing industry's place in the pipeline from fibre production to retail store. Robert Frazier in How Industry Can Deliver the Quick Response, *Apparel International*, January 1968, 9 (1) looks at this in a modern context. The structure and background of the industry is covered in: A.G. Hamlyn and G.I.W. Llewelyn (Eds) (1971) *Technology and the Garment Industry*, Programmes Analysis Unit, HMSO; *The 1980s: The Decade for Technology? A Study of the State of the Art of Assembly of Apparel Products*, prepared for the Commission of the European Economic Community, Kurt Salmon Associates (1979); *A Productivity Survey of the Ladies' and Children's Light Outerwear Section of the British Clothing Industry*, Clothing Industry Productivity Resources Agency (now The British Clothing Centre) (CIPRA) (1980).

The comparative costs of manufacturing in the USA and the Far East are covered in John J. Ullman, Productivity and human resources, *Bobbin*, February 1981, a précis of a report to the EC.

2 Design and innovation

One of the suggestive texts about the nature of design is M.J. French (1988) *Invention and Evolution: Design in Nature and Engineering*, Cambridge University Press.

Aspects of the marketing of clothing are covered in: *Planning and Implementing an Apparel Sourcing Strategy*, AAMA (1986); *Dynamic Response: How Retailers, Knitwear Manufacturers, Spinners and Dyers can Together Improve their Response to Consumer Demand*, Knitting EDC, NEDO (1987); *Changing Needs and Relationships in the UK Apparel Fabric Market*, NEDO (1982); G. Wills *et al.* (1973) *Fashion Marketing*, Allen and Unwin.

Further information is in the following articles: M.A. Hann *et al.* (1987) Fashion, an interdisciplinary approach. *Textile Progress*, **16**, 4; Caroline Marnoch (1985) A study of mail order. *Hollings Apparel Industry Review (HAIR)*, **5**, 2; Thomas N. Roboz, Government procurement in the land of Crud. *Bobbin*, June 1968, **19**, 10; Melanie Room (1984) A study of market segmentation and target marketing. *HAIR*, **1**, 1; Lesley Smout (1985) The men's rainwear scene in the UK. *HAIR*, **2**, 2; Nichola Taylor and Jeff Lowe (1984) The outsize market for men's and women's outerwear. *HAIR*, **1**, 2.

The physiological aspects of clothing are discussed in: Lyman Fourt and Norman Hollies (1970) *Clothing: Comfort and Function*, Dekker; N.R.S. Hollies and R.F. Goldman (Eds) (1977) *Clothing Comfort: Interaction of Thermal, Ventilation, Construction and Assessment Factors*, Ann Arbor Science, Ann Arbor, Michigan; E.T. Renbourne and W.H. Rees (1972) *Materials and Clothing in Health and Disease* (with *The Biophysics of Clothing Materials*), Lewis; *Textiles for Comfort*, papers presented at the third Shirley international seminar, Shirley Institute, nd; Susan M. Watkins (1986) *Clothing: The Portable Environment*, Iowa State University Press, Ames, Iowa; and Omar Sattaur (1990) Clothes for the fashionably fit. *New Scientist*, **128**, 1748/9.

The social psychology of clothing has a large literature, beginning with J. Flugel (1930) *The Psychology of Clothes*, Hogarth Press, progressing through the entertaining but now much criticized ideas of James Laver (1969) *Modesty and Dress*, Heinemann, London, and

(1937) *Taste and Fashion*, Harrop, and Mary Shaw Ryan (1966) *Clothing: A Study in Human Behaviour*, Holt, Reinhart, Winston, to Ted Polhemus (Ed.) (1978) *Fashion and Anti-Fashion*, Thames and Hudson, London. The best summary and commentary on all these ideas is Elizabeth Rouse (1989) *Understanding Fashion*, BSP Professional Books, Oxford.

A number of writers illustrate the techniques of fashion drawing. Among the most straightforward and lucid are the books by Patrick John Ireland, beginning with (1970) *Fashion Design Drawing*, Batsford, London.

The authors would not presume to make selections among the many books describing the techniques of pattern cutting, but it seems a fundamentally sound approach to relate the making of garments to the cutting of patterns, as in Martin Shoben and Janet Ward (1987) *Pattern Cutting and Making Up: The Professional Approach*, Heinemann, London. Grading is covered in Patrick J. Taylor and Martin M. Shoben (1986) *Grading for the Fashion Industry: The Theory and Practice*, Hutchinson, London, and Gerry Cooklin (1990) *Pattern Grading for Women's Clothes*, BSP Professional Books, Oxford.

The authors are grateful to Nicola Arrowsmith for permission to use material from her dissertation, *History of Corsetry in the Twentieth Century*, presented for part 2 of the Examinations of the CFI.

3 Management of the process

Charles Handy (1985) *Understanding Organisations*, Penguin, Harmondsworth. Williams (1989) *Management and Organisation*, South West Publishing Co, Dublin, Ireland.

4 Quality control

The most comprehensive coverage is Pradip V. Mehta (1985) *An Introduction to Quality Control*, JSN Inc, Tokyo. Fundamental concepts are discussed in J. Lowe and P.D. Lowcock (1986) *A Approach to Quality Control in the Clothing Industry*, Emraine Publications, Ware. See also Richard D. Sikora, Quality costs: actual case history in the garment industry. *Bobbin*, July 1969, 10 (11); R. Lumb (1975) *Reducing Costs and Maintaining Quality in Trouser Manufacture*, WIRA; and Alex Rae (1985) A collective responsibility: QC (A report by the British Clothing Centre), Part 1 April and Part 2 May. *Apparel International*, 7 (4 and 5); Dale, Plunkett (1990) *Managing Quality*, about BS 5750.

5 Materials

There are many excellent texts describing the materials and manufacture of textiles, but this book is concerned with the development of clothing products; hence the significant texts are those which relate textile properties to the manufacture, wear and after care of clothing. Tortora (1987) *Understanding Textiles*, Collier Macmillan, is a good general account.

This selection deals with particular problems: E.I. du Pont de Nemours Inc, Production hints: how to measure the elastic properties of woven stretchable fabrics. *Bobbin*, May 1976, **17** (9); Perry Ashley, Bobbin Questionnaire: fabric. *Bobbin*, April 1984, **25** (8); Kathy Osteen, Fabric performance survey results. *Bobbin*, June 1978, **19** (6); Kathryn Jakes *et al.*, A primer on seam flammability. *Bobbin*, December 1974, **16** (4); Norman Wilson, Static electricity. *Manufacturing Clothier*, February 1985, **66** (2).

An introduction to the work of Professor Kawabata and his large team of researchers worldwide is in Sueo Kawabata (1980) *The Standardisation of Hand Evaluation*, Textile Machinery Society of Japan, Osaka. Further references to the work of this team can be found under Chapter 6, Manufacture; also through an article by Fred Fortess, The Kawabata system for the standardisation and the analysis of hand. *Bobbin*, October 1982, **24** (2) which reviews the team's first symposium.

6 Manufacture

General overviews of manufacturing technology are Harold Carr and Barbara Latham (1988) *The Technology of Clothing Manufacture*, BSP Professional Books, Oxford, and the enormous book by Jacob Solinger (1980) *Apparel Manufacturing Handbook*, Van Nostrand Reinhold Co, in which about a quarter of the text refers to clothing manufacturing technology.

The British Standards Institution, Linford Wood, Milton Keynes MK14 6LE, publishes BS 3870 Part 1 1982 *Stitches and Seams, Classification of Stitch Types* and Part 2 1983 *Stitches and Seams, Classification and Terminology of Seam Types*. These standards are identical with ISO (International Organisation for Standardisation) 4915–1981 and ISO 4916–1982 as well as US Federal Standard 751a 1983. It is impossible to discuss sewing without the language and system of diagrams developed by the above organisations.

Fusing is best covered by the Bulletins of the British Interlining Manufacturers' Association (BIMA), which collectively discuss most of the issues in fusing technology: base cloths, fusible resins, testing procedures, typical garment construction applications and so on. The use and application of trims is best described in Carr and Latham, *op. cit.*, and the 'Further Reading' within it.

For embroidery there is Margaret Disher, Machine embroidery and trimming. *Manufacturing Clothier*, September 1986, 67 (9); Embroidery fashion perspective. *Bobbin*, May 1980, 21 (9); John M. Murray, The competing technologies of apparel decoration. ARJ in *Bobbin*, June 1976, 17 (10); and Colin Schneider, A general look at multi-head machines. *Bobbin*, May 1980, 21 (9).

For quilting there is the older *Quilting Guide* by George R. Donahue, Apparel Institute Inc., nd; and Barry Shore, Computer controlled scroll quilting. *Bobbin*, June 1983, 24 (10).

For pressing see Carr and Latham, *op. cit.*, and its 'Further Reading'.

For fabric evaluation see: Sueo Kawabata (Ed.) (1985) *Objective Measurement: Applications to Product Design and Process Control.* Proceedings of the third Japan–Australia joint symposium on objective measurement, Kyoto, Japan, 5–7 September, 1985. Textile Machinery Society of Japan, Osaka; Sueo Kawabata *et al.* (Eds) (1982) *Objective Specification of Fabric Quality, Mechanical Properties and Performance.* Proceedings of the Japan–Australia joint symposium, Kyoto, Japan, 10–12 May, 1982; R. Postle *et al.* (Eds) (1983) *Objective Evaluation of Apparel Fabrics.* Proceedings of the second Australia–Japan bilateral science and technology symposium on objective evaluation of apparel fabrics, Parkville, Victoria, Australia, 24 October–4 November, 1983.

The latest research information on these themes was contained in papers presented at a Textile Objective Measurement Conference UK, 1990, and reported as Textile objective measurement and automation in garment manufacture, six articles in *International Journal of Clothing Science and Technology*, 2 (3/4).

7 Costs and profits

See the following: AAMA, Product costing: new complexities. *Bobbin*, October 1985, 27 (2); A cautionary tale of marginal costing. *Women's Wear*, April 1973; Manuel Gaetan, Garment costing; method or madness. *Bobbin*, March 1978, 19 (7); I.A. Kahn, Strategies for remaining competitive when costs increase for manufacturers of fashion merchandise. *Bobbin*, September 1979, 21 (1).

For the influences on material cost, and a piece of fundamental research, see B. Trautman, *Material Utilisation in the Apparel Industry: Current Practices and Recommendations for the Future,* Apparel Research Foundation (1970) and Manchester Polytechnic (1982).

8 The costs of product development

See Inbucon/AIC (1973) *Investment Appraisal for the Clothing Industry*, HMSO; Buel S. Combs and Wallace D. Dupre, Training for style change. *Bobbin*, July 1969, **10** (10); Manuel Gaetan, The dynamic portion of the learning curve. *Bobbin*, January 1969, **10** (5).

9 Operations management

See H.C. Carr (1985) *The Organisation, Planning and Control of Production in Clothing Manufacture*, Emraine Publications, Ware, especially Chapter 5 Production Planning; Wayne Kolbeck, The Gantt chart: an old procedure re-evaluated. *Bobbin*, December 1984, **26** (4).

Relationships with suppliers are covered in Susan L. Smarr, The TALC talks (Textile/Apparel Linkage Council). *Bobbin*, July 1987, **28** (11) and Staying in tune with TALC and SAFLINC (Sundries and Apparel Findings Linkage Council). *Bobbin*, February 1988, **29** (6); and the overall organisation in Sy Mendel, MRP II part one: Kellwood's big company approach (MRP II = Manufacturing Resource Planning; the II distinguishes it from MRP = Materials Requirements Planning). *Bobbin*, February 1987, **28** (6); and MRP II part two. *Bobbin*, March 1987, **28** (7).

The authors are grateful to Jacqueline Gash for permission to use material from her dissertation *Delivery Assured*, presented for Part 2 of the CFI Examinations.

For production organisation, see H.C. Carr, *op. cit.*, Chapter 3, Sewing Room Design. For more modern organisations, see David Sinclair, Stand up and sew. *Apparel International*, July 1982, **2** (1); David Tyler, Production improvement through the 'Just-in-time' route. *Apparel International*, June 1986; Geoff Price *et al.*, Team spirit. *Manufacturing Clothier*, July 1990, **71** (7); and Anne Imperato Tray, Unit production; a systematic evaluation. *Bobbin*, Parts 1, 2 and 3, January, February and March 1986.

Index

Printed in Great Britain
by Amazon.co.uk, Ltd.,
Marston Gate.